DOC FIZZIX Mousetrap Racers
The Complete Builder's Manual

DOC FIZZIX Mousetrap Racers

The Complete Builder's Manual

Alden J. Balmer

Fox Chapel Publishing
1970 Broad Street • East Petersburg, PA 17520
www.FoxChapelPublishing.com

Illustrations by Mike Harnisch

ISBN 978-1-56523-359-1

Publisher's Cataloging-in-Publication Data

Balmer, Alden J.
      Doc Fizzix mousetrap racers : the complete builder's manual / Alden
      J. Balmer ; illustrations by Mike Harnisch. -- 1st ed. -- East
      Petersburg, PA : Fox Chapel Publishing, c2008.

            p. ; cm.
            ISBN: 978-1-56523-359-1
            Audience: Ages 10 and up.

            Summary: Build cool, fast dragsters powered by the energy of a
      wound moustrap spring, all the while discovering the fun of physics
      and engineering. Includes plans for seven different mousetrap
      racers, revealing speed and distance tricks, trouble-shooting tips
      and techniques and more.

            1. Automobiles--Models--Design and construction. 2. Toy
      making. 3. Springs (Mechanism)--Models. 4. Physics--Study and
      teaching. I. Harnisch, Mike. II. Title. III. Title: Mousetrap racers.
      IV. Title: Mouse trap racers.
TT174.5.V43 B35 2008
629.22/12--dc22   2008

To learn more about the other great books from Fox Chapel Publishing, or to find a retailer
near you, call toll free 800-457-9112 or visit us at *www.FoxChapelPublishing.com*.

Note to Authors: We are always looking for talented authors to write new books in our area
of woodworking, design, and related crafts. Please send a brief letter describing your idea to
Acquisition Editor, Fox Chapel Publishing, 1970 Broad Street, East Petersburg, PA 17520.

First Printing—August 2008

ABOUT THE AUTHOR

Doc Fizzix—Alden J. Balmer—is an award-winning physics teacher from McNeil High School in Round Rock Independent School District and the 1996 Texas Science Teacher of the Year. Doc Fizzix has appeared on several nationally aired television programs and has been featured in many magazines including: *The Science Teacher*, *Boys' Life*, *Web Page Design*, *Physics Today*, and more. While teaching, Balmer observed students had little experience working with their hands or building things. In 1990, in lieu of the traditional semester exam, Balmer had students build a mousetrap-powered racer, believing it was a great way for students to demonstrate their understanding of physics and build something on their own. Doc Fizzix has spent a lot of time traveling around the country sharing his teaching methods and activities with other science teachers. As Doc Fizzix traveled, he shared his mousetrap-racer activity with more and more groups of teachers and before long, he had people asking him for a book on the subject. He wrote *Mouse Trap Racers: The Secrets to Success* in 1995. Doc Fizzix Products opened the same year in Round Rock, Texas. His products are also available at his Website, www.docfizzix.com.

Doc Fizzix—Alden J. Balmer (right) with his wife, Carol, and their daughter, Alysse.

Acknowledgment

I want to thank my mother, Dr. Karen Ostlund, who has so unselfishly given her love to me. Without her love and support, I would never be where I am today.

The universe is an intriguing place, a place of secrets and mysteries. At times the universe reveals her secrets when she becomes a stage for the most magnificent show man has ever seen, physics. You cannot appreciate the universe until you understand the rules by which it operates! Physics shows us the rules of the universe and exposes an intriguing mathematical relationship that exist between everything. Physics satisfies our insatiable appetite for knowledge and shows as some of the mathematical relationships that determine our existence. This book is dedicated to all those who have ever attempted to learn the rules by which our universe operates.

TABLE OF CONTENTS

Introduction to Mousetrap Racers

Power a toy car with a mousetrap?

Generate ideas.

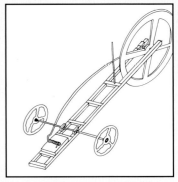

Choose One idea and build it.

In this book, you'll learn:

✔ how to get started;

✔ the most important physics concepts related to mousetrap racecars;

✔ how to build many types of racers for both speed and distance concepts; and

✔ advanced construction techniques.

For 13 years, I have been able to help students learn challenging physics concepts by teaching them to build things. I have been fortunate to share this incredible journey with my wife, Carol, and daughter, Alysse.

I was the 1996 Science Teacher of the Year in Texas and I loved teaching. But I noticed my students had very little experience building things.

So, in 1990, instead of a traditional semester exam, I had my students build mousetrap-powered racers. I believe it is more important for students to understand and apply physics than to spit out answers for a test. The students had more fun than they ever dreamed, and developed a true understanding for the concepts taught during the course.

I began making and selling Doc Fizzix merchandise in 1995. My wife and I started the company in our garage in Round Rock, Texas. By 2000, the side business demanded so much of my time that I had to leave teaching. After years of experimenting with these devices, I devised mousetrap cars that enabled the simple motion of a wound spring to propel them at exceptionally high speeds, over long distances, or up inclines. This allowed my students to see and

  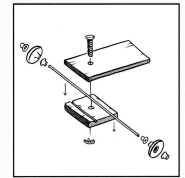

Test the car.	Experiment with one variable at a time.	Build a better car!

understand how the concepts of physics were applied. The designs have yielded long-distance racers capable of traveling more than 180 meters and speed-trap racers that have reached speeds of 5 meters in 1 second.

Also, the closing chapter contains a series of Advanced Science Labs for students with more than just a casual interest in physics and mousetrap racers. The first lab, *The Lever's Edge,* is brand new and has never appeared in print.

When you are constructing your racer, please, take care when using sharp tools. Measure twice and cut once. Lastly, wear protective equipment as recommended.

Though I share several designs in this book, there is never just one way to build a racer: there are infinite possibilities to reach the same objective. Even two racers built the same way will not necessarily perform the same.

By reading this book, you will learn *why* these models are effective and how to build new and experimental mousetrap cars yourself. Understanding the principles of motion and energy will give you new insights and levels of control over whatever type of mousetrap car or other machine you could want to construct.

Building and experimenting with machines can be challenging, but take it from an expert who has had his share of failed attempts: the most valuable lessons are those you learn from your own mistakes.

Now, get out there and create some innovative ways to build mousetrap racers!

— **Alden J. Balmer**, a.k.a. Doc Fizzix,
Red Rock, Texas, March 2008

What is a Mousetrap Racer? How Does It Work?

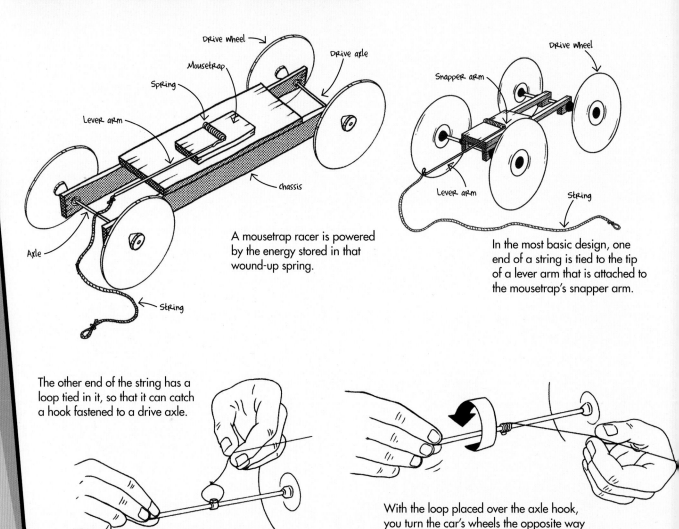

Drive wheel

Mousetrap

Spring

Drive axle

Lever arm

chassis

Axle

String

A mousetrap racer is powered by the energy stored in that wound-up spring.

Snapper arm

Drive wheel

Lever arm

String

In the most basic design, one end of a string is tied to the tip of a lever arm that is attached to the mousetrap's snapper arm.

The other end of the string has a loop tied in it, so that it can catch a hook fastened to a drive axle.

With the loop placed over the axle hook, you turn the car's wheels the opposite way to the direction you intend the car to move.

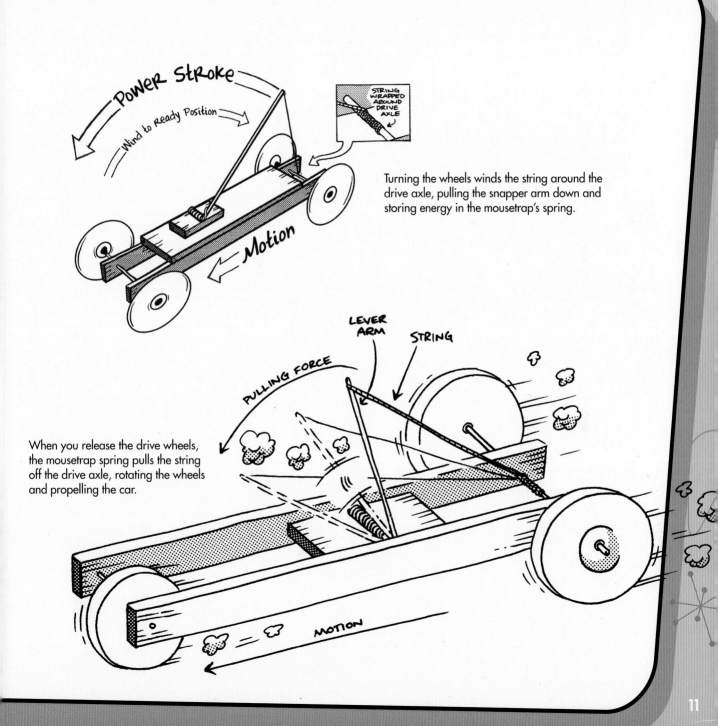

Power Stroke

Wind to Ready Position

STRING WRAPPED AROUND DRIVE AXLE

Motion

Turning the wheels winds the string around the drive axle, pulling the snapper arm down and storing energy in the mousetrap's spring.

LEVER ARM

STRING

PULLING FORCE

When you release the drive wheels, the mousetrap spring pulls the string off the drive axle, rotating the wheels and propelling the car.

MOTION

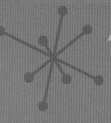

"If a man writes a better book, preach a better sermon, or make a better mousetrap than his neighbor, tho' he build his house in the woods, the world will make a beaten path to his door."
— Ralph Waldo Emerson

CHAPTER 1

"If you build a better mousetrap, you will catch better mice."
— George Gobel

"Anyone who has never made a mistake has never tried anything new."
— Albert Einstein.

Getting Started

The spring in a mousetrap is very powerful and fast. It can snap down with blinding speed, but we'll need to slow it down to a useful speed. We'll do so using the basic principles of physics.

Wind the string of a mousetrap racer and you'll store potential energy. Let the lever go and it will pull the string attached to the axle, releasing the potential energy as kinetic energy. The kinetic energy turns the axle, which then makes the wheels rotate. The rotational inertia of the wheels is converted into linear motion and your racer flies across the floor, travels a long distance, or performs another task you've created on your own.

But to get there you've got to start at the beginning.

Novice builders usually can build racers that travel several meters using the most basic design. To build racers that can travel more than 100 meters, or faster than 5 meters in under a second, the builder has to understand some of the variables that influence the racer's performance.

Building mousetrap racers provides experience in design and engineering. You start with ideas and turn them into a real racer that works. Building a mousetrap racer is an advanced form of problem solving with two main ingredients:

- You will discover and solve many of the problems in building as you progress.
- There is never one right answer to solving any one problem.

One of the major goals of the mousetrap racer program is to help students learn to think, analyze, and build. That means you should go ahead and experiment.

Be aware, though. There are trade-offs. For instance, building a racer that accelerates quickly means sacrificing fuel efficiency and traveling a shorter distance. Exaggerating one variable on the racer might seem like a good idea, but it can lead to negative performance. The best method is to find a harmonious balance through experimentation. Experiment often and early and do not worry about making mistakes. A good engineer knows one way to get something to work and 100, 200, 300, or more ways it will not work.

The Mousetrap

James Henry Atkinson of Britain invented "Little Nipper," the prototype of the five-part mousetrap, in 1897. For a relatively simple tool first constructed more than 100 years ago, it has been remarkably enduring.

American John Mast of Lititz, Pennsylvania, received a patent on his similar snap-trap mousetrap in 1899.

Mast's invention ultimately became the Victor® mousetrap that is the most commonly sold mousetrap in the United States.

It's all in the mousetrap.

Victor Mousetraps are the official mousetraps for mousetrap racers. Even though Victor is the standard, not all springs have the same strength. Even with this variation, if your goal is to build the best possible racer, use Victor™.

Victor™ Mousetraps still are manufactured in Lancaster County, Pennsylvania.

Victor™ is a registered trademark of Woodstream Corporation, 69 N. Locust St., Lititz, Pa.

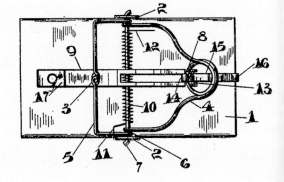

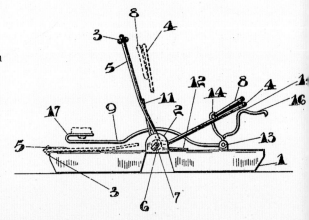

The Parts

Get to know the names of the mousetrap's parts and their functions. It will help you to stay safe as you follow the instructions in this book.

Spring
Bail
Locking Lever
WOODSTREAM CORP
USA
VICTOR
Bait Hook
Base

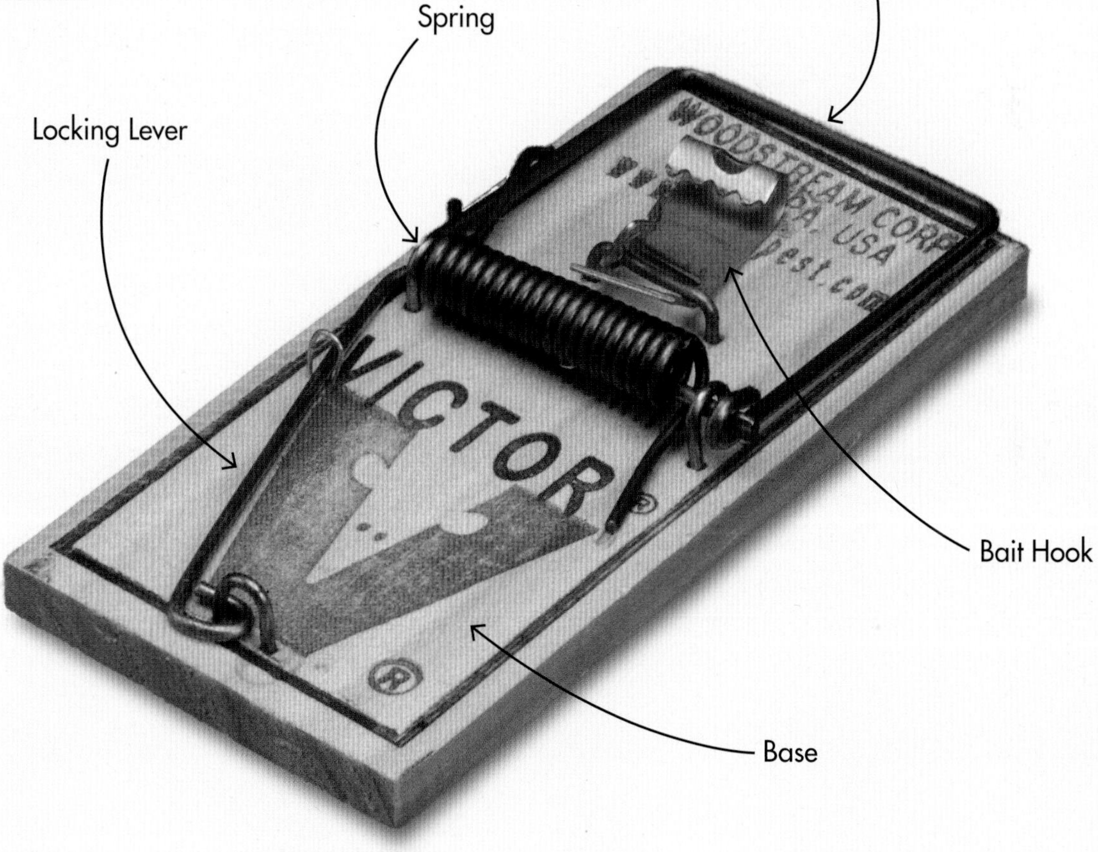

Safety

Safety is important as you construct your mousetrap racer.

First, evaluate your workplace. Is it clean, orderly, well-lit, and well-ventilated? If not, move.

Second, wear rubber or latex gloves when working with glue or lead solder. After working with lead, wash hands thoroughly. Use snug leather gloves when working with sharp tools.

Third, wear goggles or glasses when working with power tools, glues, or solder.

Fourth, use a facemask to protect against harmful fumes and airborne particles.

Fifth, to preserve your hearing, wear ear protection when running power equipment. Earplugs or earmuffs protect from loud noises as well as the intrusion of water, foreign bodies, dust, or excessive wind.

Home centers and many department stores sell latex and/or leather gloves, goggles/glasses, facemasks, and ear protection.

If you are supervising a child or assisting a teenager, discuss safety procedures—including securing loose clothing, hair, and jewelry—before using any tools, glues, or materials.

Follow the manufacturer's instructions included with any equipment or materials. No exceptions.

If you are working on your own, be sure to follow the same safety rules you would impose on anyone else working in your space.

Mousetrap springs

A mousetrap's spring is under great tension. The trap's spring-loaded bar swings down in a fraction of a second, usually when a mouse or other small rodent touches the trip. The rodent's neck or spinal cord usually is broken, or its ribs or skull crushed, by the force of the bar. The force may decapitate the rodent. If the mousetrap snaps on any finger or appendage, severe pain will result. Keep fingers and appendages clear of the mousetrap bail's landing pad. This rule applies to children, teenagers, and adults.

A mousetrap has great force—be sure to keep all fingers and appendages clear of the landing pad!

Tools You May Need

You may use a variety of tools in constructing your mousetrap racer. Be certain to review and comply with all operating instructions to reduce the chance of injuring yourself or others.

Anyone unfamiliar with the operation of any tool should consult an experienced user before embarking on a project.

You'll need a hand-held power drill for drilling holes; a rotary tool, like a Dremel,™ for cutting, sanding, and other tasks; a rotary tool chuck for changing and tightening bits; a ¼" drill bit for making holes; and a hot glue gun for gluing. You will also need ³/₈" and ³/₁₆" drill bits for some projects.

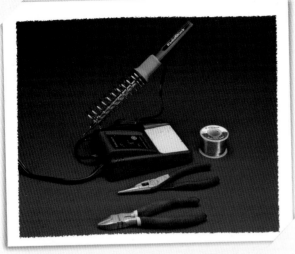

A soldering iron for optional wire soldering, needle-nose pliers for twisting wire and dissembling mousetraps, and wire cutters will all come in handy during mousetrap construction.

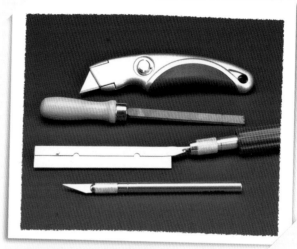

You will need a straightedge razor, such as an X-Acto™ hobby knife, for cutting your hobby wood; a hobby saw, like X-Actos, for cutting tubes; a file for smoothing rough edges; and a utility knife for various cutting tasks.

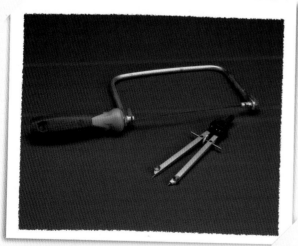

A coping saw will be used for cutting and a compass for making perfect circles.

Supplies You May Need

The exact supplies you will need to build your mousetrap racer will depend upon what type of racer you plan to build, and upon your imagination.

The supplies shown here constitute everything needed to build all types of known racers. You may use these, which are available at many hobby, hardware, craft, and department stores, or you may decide to use completely different supplies. Consult each project to determine the precise supplies needed for each.

If you are entering a contest with entry rules, be sure to consult those rules before developing plans for your unique racer.

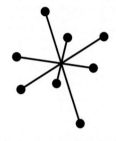

Victor brand standard mousetraps are the recommended brand of trap for official mousetrap races.

Balsa or bass hobby wood (two strips, 3" x 18" x $\frac{1}{8}$" or $\frac{3}{16}$") will be used to build the racer, along with masking tape, which is used while preparing your pieces for construction.

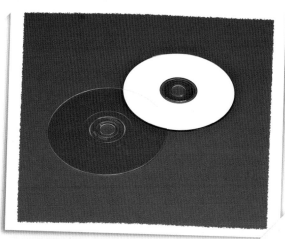

CDs or CD package inserts can be excellent wheels for your mousetrap racer.

DVDs or DVD layers (available commercially only from Docfizzix.com) also are excellent wheel choices for your racer.

Wheels from old toys, such as airplane kits, or old vinyl record albums can be another source for wheels. The type of wheels can vary from project to project.

Use wet and dry sandpaper for sanding, graphite powder for eliminating friction, and spray lubricant, such as WD-40™, for lubricating and grease removal purposes.

Mat board or cardboard are optional materials if your project is a Big Wheel Racer. Big Wheels require a wheel made of sturdy material.

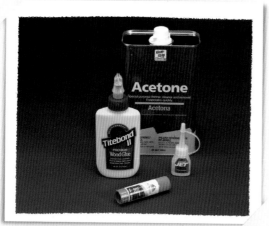

Glue: Wood glue, glue sticks, and cyanoacrylate glue, like Instant Jet Glue™, are all potential glues you can use in your construction projects. Keep some acetone—a de-bonder for cyanoacrylate glue—on hand. Always follow handling instructions and cautions for glue and de-bonder.

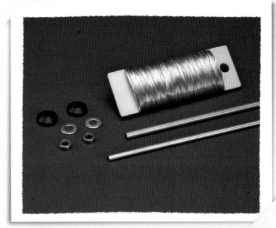

Plastic and metal washers are essential for reducing friction. Picture framer's wire can be used to construct a strong axle hook. Brass tubing, $1/8$" and $3/16$", are needed to construct most types of racer. You may also need faucet washers and $5/32$" brass tubing for some projects.

Zip ties also can be used to construct an axle hook, or to create a racer powered by two mousetraps. Kevlar™ fishing string, such as Spider Wire™, is required for all racer projects. For some models, a 10-24 bolt assembly, 4-40 1/2" socket head screws, blind nuts, or 1/4"-20 x 1" nylon bolts and nuts are required.

Kevlar™ fishing string, such as Spider Wire™, is required for all racer projects.

Facemask, goggles, latex gloves, and ear protection (to be worn when using power tools) are essential for your safety. I recommend the use of all four while you work on any mousetrap racer project.

Your challenge: A car built using a harmonious balance of tools and materials.

"A free lunch is only found in mousetraps."
— John Capozzi

CHAPTER 2

"One thing they don't tell you about doing
experimental physics is that sometimes
you must work under adverse conditions...
like a state of sheer terror."
— W. K. Hartmann

"The faster you go, the shorter you are."
— Albert Einstein

Understanding Mousetrap Racers

Many concepts of physics interact when the energy stored in a mousetrap's spring is converted into forward motion on wheels. We'll look at each concept in turn, starting with the one that has the most effect on everything: **Friction**.

Friction

Because of friction, a ball rolling across the floor will eventually slow to a stop. Friction always opposes motion. If not for friction, the ball would roll forever, as long as there was nothing, a wall for example, to stop its motion. Friction occurs any time two surfaces slip, slide, roll, or move against one another. A ball given an initial push will roll until friction consumes all of its energy, whereupon it stops. The greater the amount of friction between two surfaces, the greater the force that will be required to keep an object moving. The smaller the forces of friction against a mousetrap racer or any other moving object, the farther it can travel on its available energy supply. There are two basic types of friction: surface friction, and fluid friction or air resistance. Reducing and eliminating all forms of friction from your car is the key to racing success.

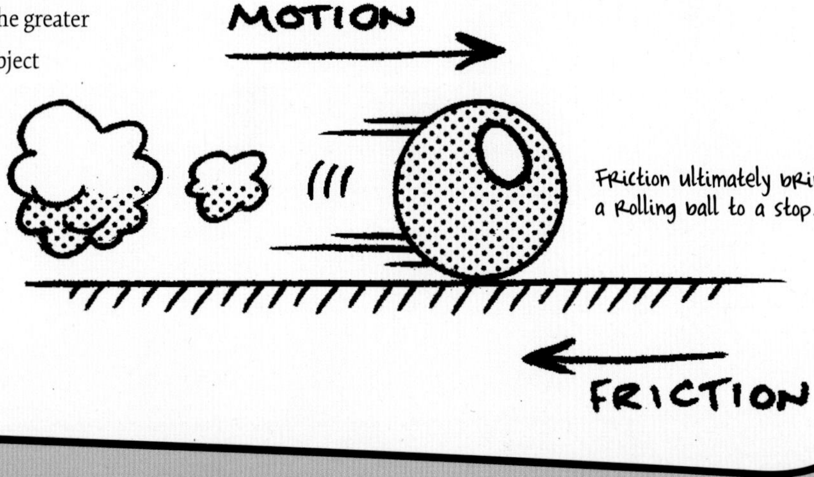

MOTION →

← FRICTION

Friction ultimately brings a rolling ball to a stop.

Surface friction

Surface friction occurs between any two surfaces that touch or rub against one another. It's caused by irregularities between the touching surfaces, which obstruct motion. Surfaces that appear very smooth are irregular when viewed microscopically.

The amount of friction between two surfaces depends on what kind of material they are made of, and how hard they are pressed together. Ice is more slippery than concrete—ice has less friction. If you have a heavy brick and a light one, the heavy brick will be harder to push because it pushes into the ground with more weight or force.

Luckily, the force of surface friction is not affected by speed. Go faster or slower, and the force of surface friction stays the same.

Minimizing surface friction on a mousetrap car allows its wheels to spin with less resistance, resulting in a car that travels faster, farther, and wastes less energy. The interface between a car's axle and its chassis is called the bearing. Surface friction always occurs in this bearing, so whether you want to build a fast racer or a distance racer, you need to reduce this friction.

An axle turning in a drilled hole is a **plain bearing**. A **bushing** is a smooth sleeve placed in the hole to give the axle a smooth rubbing surface. Brass and plastic are good materials for bushings, but aluminum is not.

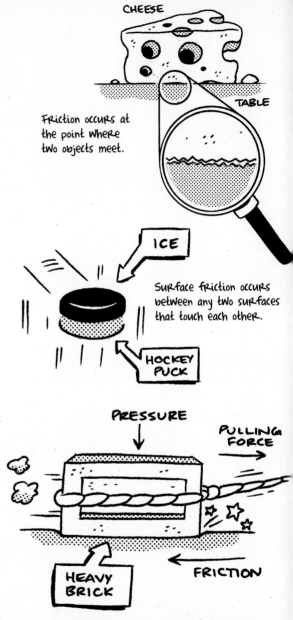

CHEESE

TABLE

Friction occurs at the point where two objects meet.

ICE

Surface friction occurs between any two surfaces that touch each other.

HOCKEY PUCK

PRESSURE

PULLING FORCE

HEAVY BRICK

FRICTION

The objects of the materials and the pressure impacting them impact the effect of surface friction.

A **ball bearing** allows the axle to roll on smooth steel balls instead of sliding in a sleeve. A rolling ball has very little friction, so ball bearings will deliver top performance, but they are also expensive and tricky to install. For more on different kinds of bearings, see page 94.

We've seen that speed doesn't affect friction, but weight does, and so do axle size and wheel diameter. A thicker diameter axle or bearing will stop turning sooner than a thinner axle or smaller bearing. Smaller diameter axles and bearings translate into better performance. Although the force of friction is the same on the surface of a large or small diameter axle, the distance where the friction occurs from the center of the axle is not the same. This is the concept of torque, which we'll discuss on page 36.

Lubricants such as graphite and oil reduce surface friction and help moving parts slide against one another with less energy loss. Here is a quick experiment: try rubbing your hands together lightly and quickly. Your hands become warm, because friction turns some of the rubbing energy into heat. Now put a small amount of lotion onto your hands and try the experiment again. Notice that your hands do not become as hot, and it is easier to move them against one another.

Different lubricants work better with different materials. Oil and grease are used between metal-on-metal surfaces. Oils do not work as well between metal-on-wood parts, but graphite powder does. Lubricants can actually increase friction with slow-moving, long-distance mousetrap cars. This is because the lubricant sticks to itself, and requires additional force to break free and start moving. Experiment with different lubricants, such as WD-40,™ Dura-Lube,™ Slick 50™ and graphite, and observe their effects.

FRICTION POINTS BETWEEN AXLE AND FRAME

On a mousetrap racer, the most common area of surface friction is between the axle and the chassis.

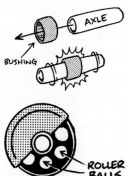
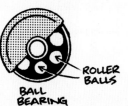

AXLE

BUSHING

ROLLER BALLS

BALL BEARING

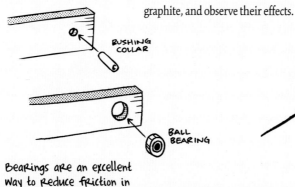

BUSHING COLLAR

BALL BEARING

Bearings are an excellent way to reduce friction in your mousetrap racer.

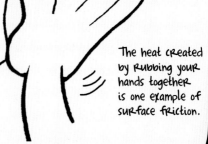

The heat created by rubbing your hands together is one example of surface friction.

Fluid friction

Friction also occurs in liquids and gases, which are called fluids. Fluid friction depends on the nature of the liquid or gas. For example, fluid friction is greater in water than it is in air. But unlike surface friction, fluid friction does depend on the speed, and also on the contact area. This makes sense—the amount of fluid pushed aside by a boat or an airplane depends on its size and shape. A slow-moving boat or airplane encounters less friction than a fast-moving one, and a wide vehicle must push aside more fluid than narrower ones.

The shape of a moving object, called its **aerodynamic**, determines how easily a fluid flows around it. Fast cars are shaped to cut through the air with less friction. Trucks have a special cowling that allows air to flow easily over the trailer. Fish have aerodynamic shapes that allow them to move easily through the water. Better aerodynamics saves energy.

The amount of fluid friction or air resistance depends on both the speed and the shape of the moving object. The force of air resistance increases with speed, an effect you can easily demonstrate by extending your arm through the open window of a moving car. The faster the car is traveling, the more air resistance you will feel. Turn your hand and test the air resistance to different aerodynamic shapes. Fast-moving mousetrap cars encounter high air resistance, causing them to use more energy and come to rest sooner than a similarly built but slower-moving car. Good aerodynamics improves the performance of any vehicle.

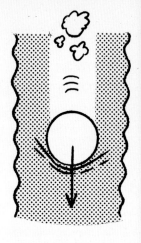

The size and shape of an object both influence the amount of air or fluid friction it faces.

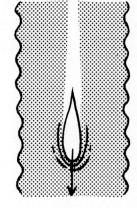

A tear drop is the most aerodynamic shape, cutting through the air with the least amount of air resistance, much like the wing of an airplane.

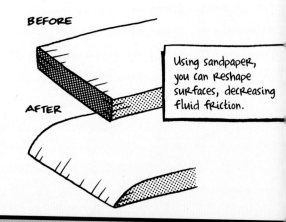

BEFORE

AFTER

Using sandpaper, you can reshape surfaces, decreasing fluid friction.

Good aerodynamics means your mousetrap car must be smooth with few or no points of air drag. Inspect the body for flat surfaces on leading edges that could catch air and increase drag. Rounding the leading edges of your vehicle will allow for smoother air movement. Cars made of wood should be sanded smooth. Tires should be thin because they are more aerodynamic than wide tires, but that is not the only consideration when it comes to choosing wheels. You must consider the number of wheels, wheel diameter and alignment (page 31), and tire traction (page 30)—all of which are governed by the forces of friction.

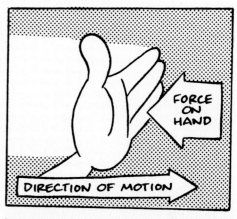

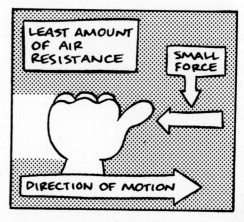

To see how much force the air can have, try the following experiment next time you are in a car.

Carefully hold your hand out the window. Try holding your hand so that your thumb points toward the sky and then try holding your hand so that your thumb points toward the direction of travel.

You will have a better understanding of fluid friction after this experiment.

A demonstration of fluid friction.

Traction

Friction is not always a bad thing. As you walk forward, the friction between the ground and your feet provides the grip you need to move. Without friction you could not move anywhere. Similarly, the friction between the road and your tires keeps the wheels from slipping and allows your vehicle to move. This type of friction is called traction.

We have already seen that thin tires offer less air resistance than wide ones, but what about knobby tires or smooth tires? Knobby tires have good traction on rough surfaces, but they are inefficient and use more energy than smooth wheels. This is because the weight of the car puts pressure directly on a knob, compressing the tire. The energy it takes to compress the tire and the air inside it is lost as heat. On mousetrap cars, smooth tires will be more energy efficient and will allow the vehicle to go farther.

Compressed knobs apply extra pressure, which generates more heat, wasting energy.

KNOB

TIRE

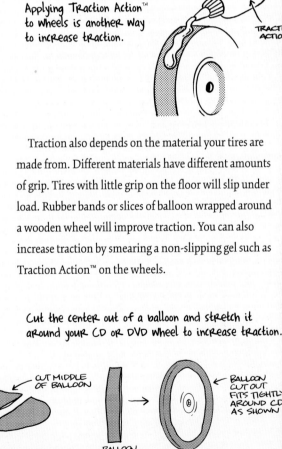

Stretching a rubber band around a wheel can increase traction.

RUBBER BAND

Applying Traction Action™ to wheels is another way to increase traction.

TRACTIC ACTION

Traction also depends on the material your tires are made from. Different materials have different amounts of grip. Tires with little grip on the floor will slip under load. Rubber bands or slices of balloon wrapped around a wooden wheel will improve traction. You can also increase traction by smearing a non-slipping gel such as Traction Action™ on the wheels.

Cut the center out of a balloon and stretch it around your CD or DVD wheel to increase traction.

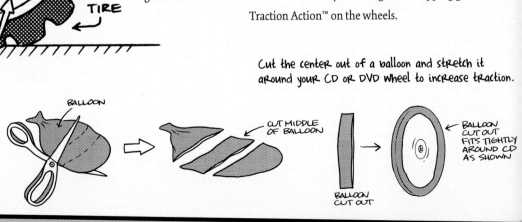

BALLOON

CUT MIDDLE OF BALLOON

BALLOON CUT OUT

BALLOON CUT OUT FITS TIGHTLY AROUND CD AS SHOWN

Wheel Considerations

The number of wheels on your vehicle does not affect the total friction. Vehicles with three wheels have fewer bearings than vehicles with four wheels. However, the vehicle's weight is distributed over three wheels rather than four, putting more pressure on each bearing and increasing the friction. The decrease in the number of bearings is offset by the increased pressure on each. It's a wash, you get no change.

However, there is another advantage to using fewer wheels: it's easier to align the wheels so they all steer in the same direction.

Vehicles turn off a straight line because of wheel alignment: the wheels are not all pointing in the same direction. Building a vehicle that travels straight is always challenging, especially with a distance vehicle because the smallest misalignment will be exaggerated over a long distance.

Vehicles turn because wheels use friction to push to one side or the other. When a wheel is turned to the left, the ground actually pushes the car in this direction. If the frictional force is not large enough to overcome the momentum of the vehicle (think of a car traveling fast on ice), the vehicle does not make the turn. If your car turns to one side, you must realign the wheels in the direction opposite the turn. It's important to test your car under operating conditions, don't just push it to see if it travels straight.

Wheel diameter can be very important on a distance car: bigger is better. When considering wheel diameter think about the following: the more rotations that a wheel makes around an axle, the greater the loss of energy to friction. Over the same measured distance, a larger diameter wheel will make fewer rotations when compared to a smaller diameter wheel; therefore, larger diameter wheels on distance vehicles reduce energy loss to friction compared to smaller wheels.

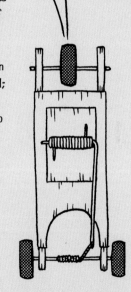

MOST ENERGY EFFICIENT

ENERGY LOST

FRICTION CAUSES TURN

PROPER steering alignment is important to the success of your mousetrap racer.

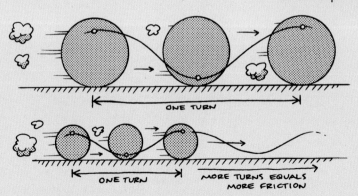

ONE TURN

ONE TURN

MORE TURNS EQUALS MORE FRICTION

Large wheels cover more distance than small ones while losing the same amount of energy to friction.

Energy

Energy has the ability to do work. Without energy the universe would be motionless and lifeless. All of the energy in the universe follows one basic rule, the **Law of Conservation of Energy**: Energy cannot be created or destroyed. It may be transformed from one form into another, but the total amount of energy never changes. We don't see energy itself, but we see it acting on objects, and being transformed.

When you wind the spring on your mousetrap car, you store potential energy in the spring. When you release the spring the car begins to move: the stored potential energy transforms into kinetic energy. Potential energy is stored energy that has the potential to do work. Kinetic energy is the energy of motion. A moving car has kinetic energy.

When building mousetrap cars, the objective is to transform the stored energy of the spring into forward motion. Two variables govern performance: friction and energy. Friction is what slows and stops your car; energy is what moves it forward. To overcome friction, you have to do work. Friction converts energy into heat and sound, causing the moving car to run out of energy and roll to a stop.

To improve your car's performance, evaluate every moving component and decrease the friction at every point. In any machine, more moving parts means more friction and as a result, higher energy consumption.

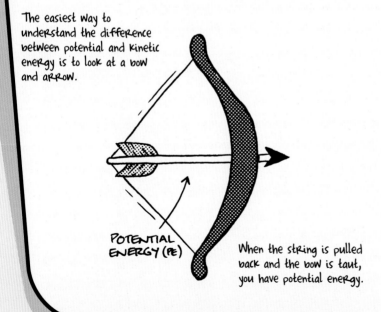

The easiest way to understand the difference between potential and kinetic energy is to look at a bow and arrow.

POTENTIAL ENERGY (PE)

When the string is pulled back and the bow is taut, you have potential energy.

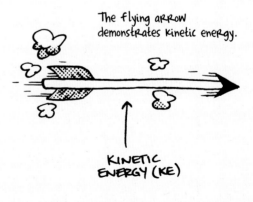

The flying arrow demonstrates kinetic energy.

KINETIC ENERGY (KE)

That's why simpler machines with few moving parts are more efficient than complex ones.

When you want to build a fast car, pay attention to reducing bearing friction and increasing traction, and also to reducing fluid friction (air resistance). This means making a smooth and aerodynamic shape. Fluid friction increases with speed. When you want to build a distance car, remember that traveling slowly encounters less air resistance. Slow cars go farther than fast ones.

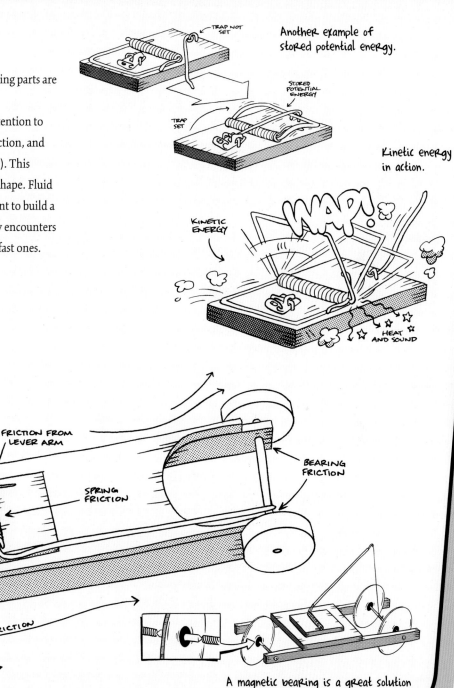

TRAP NOT SET

Another example of stored potential energy.

STORED POTENTIAL ENERGY

TRAP SET

Kinetic energy in action.

KINETIC ENERGY

WAP!

HEAT AND SOUND

There are many friction points on a mousetrap Racer

FRICTION FROM LEVER ARM

AIR FRICTION

SPRING FRICTION

BEARING FRICTION

BEARING FRICTION

AIR FRICTION

A magnetic bearing is a great solution to beating friction.

Here Are The Rules

Everything we've been discussing—force, energy, friction—is ruled by three **Laws of Motion**, which were discovered by Sir Isaac Newton during the seventeenth century.

Newton's First Law of Motion: Every material object continues in its state of rest or in uniform motion in a straight line unless it is compelled to change that state by forces acting on it. In other words, objects have inertia, which means they resist change in motion. Newton's first law is often called The Law of Inertia.

Mass is the numerical measurement of inertia. Weight is related to mass but is not the same thing: weight is the measurement of mass being pulled by gravity. Because the force of gravity on the Earth is six times higher than on the Moon, a bowling ball weighs six times as much when it is on the Earth as on the Moon. But if you were to heft the ball and throw it on either planet, it would feel the same. That's because the mass of the bowling ball does not change, and that's what you are working against, not its weight.

When you want to change how an object is moving, you have to apply a force. Applying a force causes the object to change its state of motion, or to accelerate. Newton wrote the Second Law of Motion to explain force, mass and acceleration.

Mass is the numerical measurement of inertia. Weight relates to mass and inertia but is not the same thing. Weight is a product of the amount of mass an object has and the amount of gravity pulling on the mass. Consider a bowling ball. On Earth, you can feel the weight of a bowling ball as you hold it to your side. If you held the bowling ball on the moon, it would feel a lot lighter because the moon's gravity is not as strong as the earth's gravity, so the bowling ball's moon weight is less than its Earth weight. If you compared throwing the bowling ball down an Earth bowling lane and one on the moon, you would find no apparent difference in force or feel because the bowling ball's mass is the same in each location. When you throw a bowling ball, you are working against its inertia, not its weight.

Newton's Second Law of Motion: The acceleration of an object is directly proportional to the force acting on the object and inversely proportional to the object's mass.

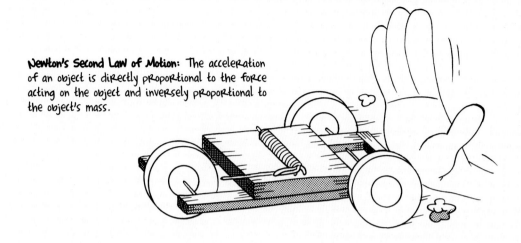

Newton's Second Law of Motion states the acceleration of an object is directly proportional to the net force acting on the object, and is inversely proportional to the mass of the object. In other words, mass resists change or acceleration, and force causes acceleration. If you want to double an object's acceleration, you have to double the pushing or pulling force. If you can't increase the force and you still want more acceleration, then you have to remove mass.

Newton's Third Law of Motion states for every action there is an equal and opposite reaction. A force is a push or a pull. Newton recognized that a force actually is an interaction between two objects. When you push on an object, the object pushes right back on you. When you push on a wall, the wall pushes back on you. Since neither you nor the wall moves, the wall has to be pushing back on you with the same force you are applying to it.

Newton's Third Law of Motion:
Pick a wall; any wall. You and the wall are an interactive pair. You apply a force to the wall and the wall applies a force back. The evidence is your bent fingers. You cannot apply force to any object without that object doing the same back to you.

You cannot push any harder than something pushes back.

Newton Builds Your Car

Because of Newton's laws, big and heavy cars (more mass) are harder to get moving than lighter (less massive) ones. Whether you are building a car for speed or for distance, it's best to build it as light as possible. Light cars not only will be easier than heavy ones to start moving, but also will have less bearing friction. However, there is always a trade-off: a car that is too light will not have enough traction to accelerate quickly.

The perfect amount of mass lies somewhere between too heavy and too light. But the only way to find it is by experimenting.

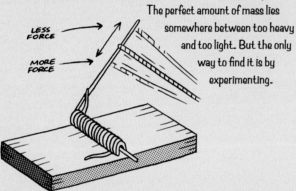

LESS FORCE
MORE FORCE

You can adjust the pulling force by attaching the string to different points on the lever arm. When you change the string attachment point, you must also adjust the position of the mousetrap from the pulling axle.

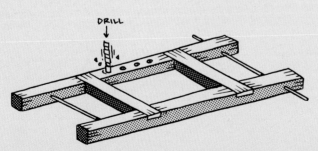

DRILL

You can improve the performance of your mousetrap racer by removing mass from the frame by drilling holes.

Torque

When you turn a water faucet, open a door, or tighten a nut with a wrench, you exert a turning force called torque. In each of these examples, the turning force is applied at a distance from the center of rotation. That distance, called the lever arm, determines the amount of leverage or mechanical advantage.

Door knobs are on the opposite edge from the hinges. This produces a lot of leverage, so it takes less force to open the door. You would have a hard time if the knob were on the hinge side! Torque is the product of the lever arm and the rotational force.

EASY

HARD!

Pick a door; any door. Pulling or pushing on the handle applies torque to a door. The torque causes the door to open or close by rotating on its hinges. To move the door, a force applied closer to the hinges will need to be larger than a force applied further from the hinges. However, the amount of torque at both locations is the same because torque is a combination of the force applied and distance it is applied from the hinge or pivot.

TIE STRING ABOVE THE DRIVE AXLE

The longer the length of the lever arm, the more string you can wind around the drive axle.

Torque is greatest when the rotational force is applied at a right angle to the radius of the object being turned. That's why, in a mousetrap car, the pulling string should be tied to the lever arm directly above the drive axle. If the lever arm extends beyond the axle in the lowered position, make it shorter or move the mousetrap farther away.

For distance cars, the longer the lever arm, the more string you can wind around the axle, and the farther the car could go. The tradeoff for a long lever arm is less pulling force. You can reduce the pulling force needed by reducing friction throughout the system. For speed cars, the shorter the lever arm, the more power will be transmitted to the drive axle, and the faster the car could go. But if you transmit too much power at the start, the wheels might just spin and slip, and you'll have to make the lever arm longer again.

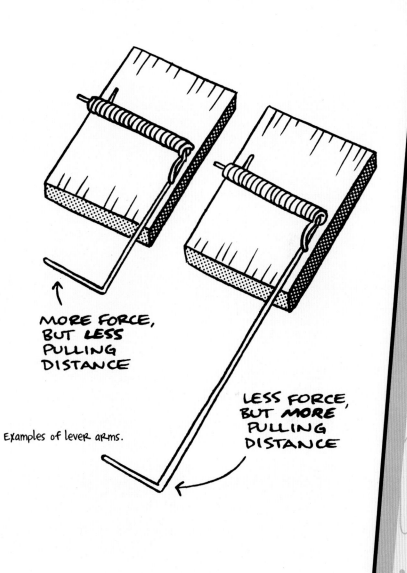

MORE FORCE, BUT **LESS** PULLING DISTANCE

LESS FORCE, BUT **MORE** PULLING DISTANCE

Examples of lever arms.

Mechanical advantage

Mechanical advantage is a number comparing the force you put into a machine with the force you get out of it.

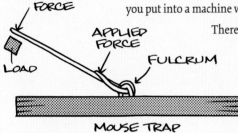

RESULTANT FORCE
APPLIED FORCE
FULCRUM
LOAD
MOUSE TRAP

A mousetrap is a third-class lever.

There is always a trade-off: if you increase the force, you reduce the distance over which it acts. That's because you can only ever get the same total amount of energy out of a machine that you put into it, and furthermore, here in the real world you will always lose some of the energy to friction.

To understand mechanical advantage, consider a lever. A mousetrap is a lever. Like all levers, it has four important elements: the applied or input force, the resultant or output force, the load, and the fulcrum. The load is what the machine is doing work on, and the fulcrum is where the lever pivots. You can change the mechanical advantage by changing the position of the applied force, load, and fulcrum.

When the mechanical advantage is greater than 1, it means the input force is smaller than the output force, and the input force is applied over a greater distance than the load travels. When the mechanical advantage is less than 1, the input force is greater than the output force, and it is applied over a smaller distance than the load travels.

In a mousetrap car, changing the diameter of either the wheel or of the axle changes the mechanical advantage. You can determine the mechanical advantage by dividing the length of string used per turn of the wheel (the size of the axle) by the distance traveled per turn of the wheel. When this ratio is less than 1, the mechanical advantage is small and the car travels slow but far. When the ratio is greater than 1, the car accelerates quickly and travels fast, but might not go as far.

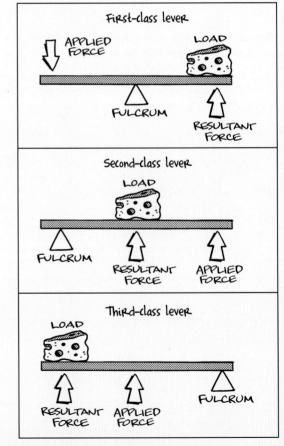

First-class lever
APPLIED FORCE
LOAD
FULCRUM
RESULTANT FORCE

Second-class lever
LOAD
FULCRUM
RESULTANT FORCE
APPLIED FORCE

Third-class lever
LOAD
RESULTANT FORCE
APPLIED FORCE
FULCRUM

Transmission

The string tied to the lever arm and wrapped around the drive axle transmits the pulling force from the mousetrap spring to the car's wheels. This system constitutes the vehicle's transmission. In addition to transferring energy from one place to another, the transmission can be used to trade speed for torque or torque for speed.

Everyone who has ridden a multi-gear bicycle understands mechanical advantage. In high gear, with the smallest gear on the rear axle, the bike goes fast on a level road but it's tough to pedal uphill. In low gear, with the largest axle pulley, you can't go fast on a level road but it's much easier to pedal uphill.

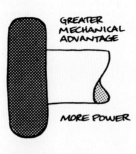

GREATER MECHANICAL ADVANTAGE

MORE POWER

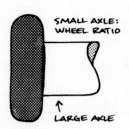

SMALL AXLE: WHEEL RATIO

LARGE AXLE

Use a small wheel-to-axle ratio with speed vehicles.

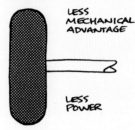

LESS MECHANICAL ADVANTAGE

LESS POWER

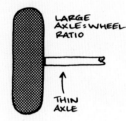

LARGE AXLE: WHEEL RATIO

THIN AXLE

Use a large wheel-to-axle ratio with distance vehicles.

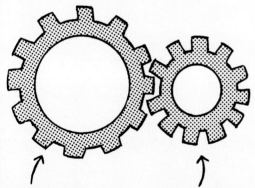

Large gears vs. small gears.

If large gear is the driver:
- Less mechanical advantage
- More speed
- Less torque

If the small gear is the driver:
- Greater mechanical advantage
- Less speed
- More torque

Mechanical advantage can be described by the ratio of the diameters of the driving pulley or gear and the driven pulley or gear. In a direct-drive mousetrap car, the driving pulley is the axle, and the driven pulley is the wheel mounted on it. For a given wheel diameter, a large-diameter axle produces high mechanical advantage and more torque. A small-diameter axle produces low mechanical advantage and less torque. For a long-distance car, you want a small force over a long distance. Therefore, use a large wheel with a small axle (a large wheel-to-axle ratio). For a fast car, you want a large force over a small distance. Therefore, use a small wheel with a large axle (a small wheel-to-axle ratio).

To test our mousetrap car, wind the spring and place the car on the ground. If the lever arm does not pull off

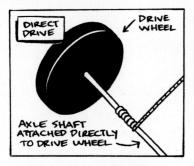

DIRECT DRIVE

DRIVE WHEEL

AXLE SHAFT ATTACHED DIRECTLY TO DRIVE WHEEL →

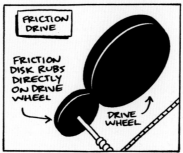

FRICTION DRIVE

FRICTION DISK RUBS DIRECTLY ON DRIVE WHEEL →

DRIVE WHEEL

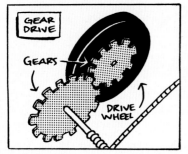

GEAR DRIVE

GEARS

DRIVE WHEEL

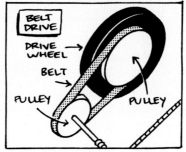

BELT DRIVE

DRIVE WHEEL

BELT

PULLEY

PULLEY

The impact of various types of drives.

the start or stops part-way through its motion, you need more torque. You can increase torque by making the lever arm shorter, using smaller diameter drive wheels, or a larger diameter drive axle. You can increase the diameter of the drive axle by wrapping tape around it. It's also possible to design a variable transmission for a mousetrap car: a tapered axle can be used to distribute larger forces at the start, with less force once the car is in motion.

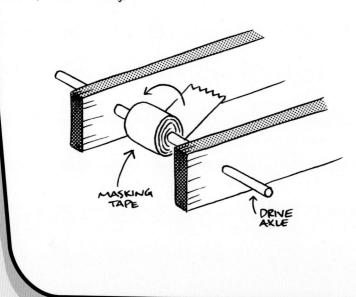

MASKING TAPE

DRIVE AXLE

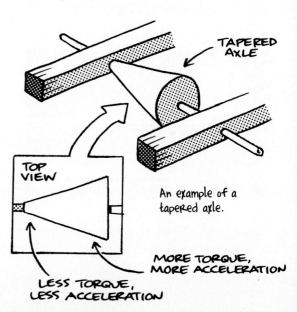

TAPERED AXLE

An example of a tapered axle.

TOP VIEW

MORE TORQUE, MORE ACCELERATION

LESS TORQUE, LESS ACCELERATION

Power

Power is the rate at which energy moves through the system. Whether you walk up the stairs or run, you do the same amount of work. However, by running you do the work faster, which means you use more power.

Variables you can adjust include where the string attaches to the lever arm, the diameter of the drive axle, and the diameter of the drive wheels. Changing any of these changes the mechanical advantage of the system and changes its power output.

When you build a mousetrap car for speed, you want maximum power output, up to just before the wheels spin out on the floor. Maximum power output means high acceleration, which you can achieve with a short lever arm, or a small axle on a large wheel.

When you build a mousetrap car for distance, you want to minimize power output, down to just before the car stalls. Minimum power output means low acceleration, which you can achieve with a long lever arm, or a large axle on a small wheel. The lower the output power, the less wasted energy and the most efficiency.

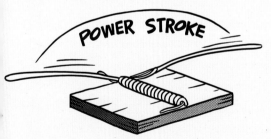

POWER STROKE

Changing the mechanical advantage of your racer's system changes its power output.

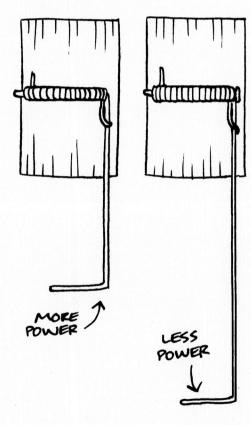

MORE POWER

LESS POWER

For speed, seek maximum power output. For distance, minimize power output.

Motion

Motion occurs all around us yet it is hard to describe and explain. We use the terms speed, velocity, and acceleration.

Speed is the measure of how fast something is traveling, that is how far it goes in a given amount of time, as in miles per hour. When you calculate the speed of a mousetrap racer, you begin timing at some predetermined starting point and then you stop timing at some measured distance away. This gives you the car's average speed over the distance.

In everyday conversation we use speed and velocity interchangeably, but they are different because velocity also includes direction. To say a car is traveling 55 miles per hour is to give its speed. To say it is going 55 miles per hour due north is to give its velocity.

An object's velocity changes when there is a change in speed, or a change in direction, or both. The rate at which velocity changes is called acceleration. A car accelerates when it goes faster or slower in a straight line, and also when it makes a turn without changing speed. In both of those situations, you can feel acceleration.

Momentum

Because of Newton's First Law of Motion (page 34), when an object is moving it tends to keep moving. We say it has momentum, which can be measured as the product of the object's velocity (above) and its mass (page 34). Although a distance car makes best use of its stored energy (page 32) by being light, a heavy car also can perform well due to its momentum. Heavy cars are harder to start because of their inertia (page 34), but once you get a heavy car moving it can coast farther than a lighter car.

To start a heavy car, you'll need to increase the pulling force by using a shorter lever arm on the mousetrap. When you use momentum you are counting on coasting distance, not pulling distance. The car won't be pulled as far as lighter and slower cars with longer lever arms, but it will get going faster. The tradeoff for that is greater air resistance. In most cases, this consumes more energy and the heavy car won't go as far as a light, slow-moving car.

Rotational Inertia

Another version of Newton's First Law of Motion says that an object rotating about an axis (such as a wheel) tends to continue rotating there, unless an external force acts upon it. This property, which resembles momentum, is called rotational inertia. Rotational inertia depends not only on the object's mass, but also on the location of the mass with respect to the axis of rotation. The farther the mass is from the axis of rotation, the greater the rotational inertia.

Whether you are building a mousetrap car for speed or for distance, it's best to use wheels with minimum rotational inertia. The less rotational inertia, the less force it will take to rotate the wheels. This means it is best to choose lightweight wheels, then make them spoked by removing mass. Cutting away mass will improve performance for both speed and distance.

This is why store-bought wheels are not the best solution. Some of the best wheels can be made from compact disks, Styrofoam™ can lids, vinyl records, and mat board.

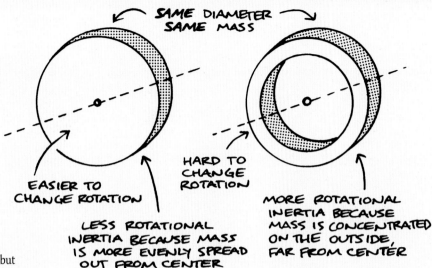

SAME DIAMETER
SAME MASS

EASIER TO
CHANGE ROTATION

HARD TO
CHANGE
ROTATION

LESS ROTATIONAL
INERTIA BECAUSE MASS
IS MORE EVENLY SPREAD
OUT FROM CENTER

MORE ROTATIONAL
INERTIA BECAUSE
MASS IS CONCENTRATED
ON THE OUTSIDE,
FAR FROM CENTER

Center of Mass

Wobbly wheels waste energy and decrease a car's performance. A wheel wobbles when it is not balanced, that is, when its center of mass is not in the center of the axle. The center of mass is simply the average position of all the mass in the object. For symmetrical objects such as a ball or a book, this point usually is at the geometrical center. For an irregular object such as a baseball bat, the center of mass is nearer to one end. You can find it by finding the bat's balance point. When an object's center of mass is located directly above the support, the object will balance.

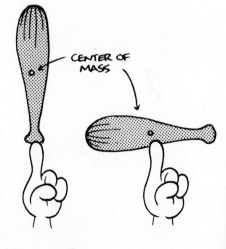

CENTER OF
MASS

Larger wheels are more affected by an offset center of mass than smaller ones. It's even possible for a distance car with an unstable wheel to roll backward after stopping. Thus, it's always best to balance a large wheel, forcing the center of mass to be located through the axle. To balance the wheel, hold it by the axle and allow it to turn freely. The heavier side will drift to the bottom. Mark it, add mass such as a blob of clay to the opposite side, and see if it continues to rotate. Repeat until the wheel no longer rotates when suspended freely by its axle.

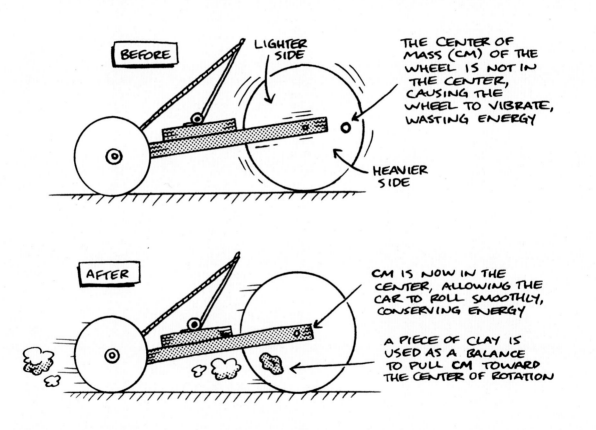

BEFORE

LIGHTER SIDE

THE CENTER OF MASS (CM) OF THE WHEEL IS NOT IN THE CENTER, CAUSING THE WHEEL TO VIBRATE, WASTING ENERGY

HEAVIER SIDE

AFTER

CM IS NOW IN THE CENTER, ALLOWING THE CAR TO ROLL SMOOTHLY, CONSERVING ENERGY

A PIECE OF CLAY IS USED AS A BALANCE TO PULL CM TOWARD THE CENTER OF ROTATION

Weight Distribution

It wastes energy when the drive wheels slip at the start. This is most likely to happen with a light-weight, high-powered car designed for speed. The remedies are to increase traction (page 40), and reduce the torque on the drive axle (page 36). The problem might also be caused by unbalanced weight distribution.

You probably know that front-wheel drive cars are better in snow than rear-wheel models. This is because the engine is directly above the drive wheels, helping increase their traction. Similarly, the balance point of your car, which represents its center of mass, should be as close as possible to the drive wheels. If your car continues to slip at the start, try adding some lumps of clay to the chassis over or near the drive wheels. Your car will press harder on the ground, increasing traction and improving its acceleration.

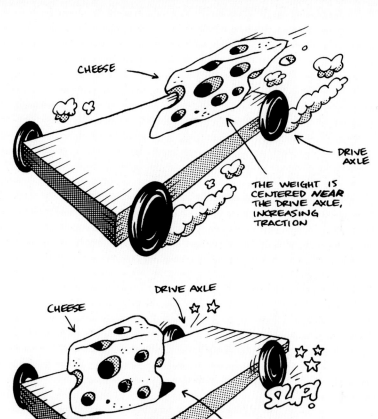

CHEESE

DRIVE AXLE

THE WEIGHT IS CENTERED *NEAR* THE DRIVE AXLE, INCREASING TRACTION

DRIVE AXLE

CHEESE

SLIP!

THE WEIGHT IS CENTERED *AWAY* FROM THE DRIVE AXLE WHICH CAUSES SLIPPING

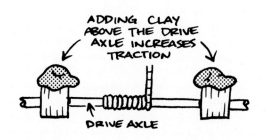

ADDING CLAY ABOVE THE DRIVE AXLE INCREASES TRACTION

DRIVE AXLE

Mousetrap racer contests

Many types of contests exist for your mousetrap racer. The type of competition you enter determines the type of racer you build.

Common types of contests:

Long-Distance Traveler

Build a mousetrap-powered racer that will travel the greatest linear distance.

Speed-Trap Racer

Build a mousetrap-powered racer that will travel a 5 m linear distance in the shortest amount of time.

King of the Hill

Build a mousetrap-powered racer that will travel the greatest linear distance up a 30° inclined ramp.

'Keep on Trucking' Challenge

Build a mousetrap-powered racer that will travel the greatest linear distance while carrying a full 12-fl. oz. soda can as cargo.

Circle Rounders

Build a mousetrap-powered racer that will travel around a 1 m diameter circle in the shortest amount of time.

There-and-Back Racers

Build a mousetrap-powered racer that will travel a five-meter distance and then back in the shortest amount of time.

Definitions:

A **racer** is a device with wheels or runners used to carry something (e.g., racer, bus, bicycle or sled). No extra part or parts of the racer may be left at the start line or along its travel path. (Launching a marble from the mousetrap, for instance, will be ruled illegal.)

Double-the-Fun Racers

Build a racer powered by two mousetraps that will travel the greatest linear distance.

Braking Racer

Build a mousetrap-powered racer that will travel five meters in the shortest time and then stop as close as possible to, but without going past, the finish line.

Common regulations

1. The mousetrap spring must be the sole source of power.

2. Do not alter the mousetrap's spring to adjust and/or change its original spring coefficient.

3. Do not change the mousetrap's base. There is one possible exception—drilling holes in the four corners to mount the mousetrap to a chassis.

4. Change the length of the bail mechanism (the snapper bar) by cutting or replacing it.

5. The racer must be self-starting and travel on its own power.

6. Most contests prohibit winding the spring beyond 180°.

7. The racer must steer itself.

8. The locking bar and bait hook may be removed.

9. The contest director has the final decision as to any changes in the rules. The contest director may inspect any racer and disqualify it if it does not follow the spirit of the contest. The contest director determines what "spirit of the contest" means.

Appendix

1. Perform contests on a smooth level floor, such as a gymnasium, a non-carpeted hallway, or at a local mall.

2. For timing accuracy, use a laser/photo-eye system. Note: Tripping photo-eye systems often require flags. (Accuracy prohibits stopwatch timing.)

3. For any climbing contest, use the following ramp specifications: 4' x 8' smooth, finish-grade plywood, arranged and supported at a 30° angle, with a 1" x 2" piece of wood attached to the lower end to establish a starting block. A 4' ramp extension is acceptable to allow teams to achieve maximum distance. Support the ramp at several points to prevent sagging.

CHAPTER 3

Mousetrap Racer Projects

Little Moe
Page 52

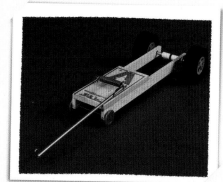

Basic Racer I
Page 74

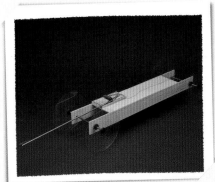

Basic Racer II
Page 84

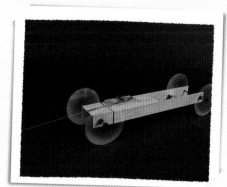

Speed-Trap Racer
Page 64

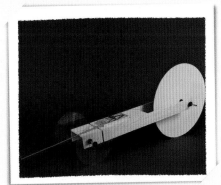

Big Wheel Racer
Page 100

A word about wheels

Throughout this book you will see a variety of wheels used, including DVDs, CDs and DVD layers. All have benefits and disadvantages that vary with the goals you have for your mousetrap racer. DVD layers have half of the thickness and rotational inertia of a normal CD, as well as much less air friction, meaning racers using them require less pulling force. This translates into an increase in travel distance between 5 to 15 m (about $5\frac{1}{2}$ to $16\frac{1}{3}$ yd) more than with CDs: more of the mousetrap's energy goes into forward motion rather than rotational motion of the wheels.

Depending on your plans, the purpose of your racer, and the contest rules, other types of wheels can be used, including wheels from Pinewood Derby racers, wheels from toy airplane kits, wheels cut from mat board, or coffee can lids.

The goal is for you to experiment and find the best wheel to suit your racer. Experimentation is what science is all about.

Old vinyl record albums as well as wheels for old toys are also options to explore for your mousetrap racer.

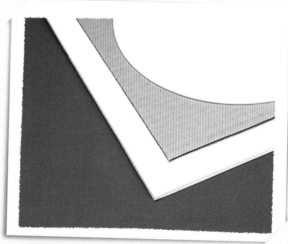

Cardboard, mat board, foam board, or other rigid lightweight materials make excellent choices for constructing a Big Wheel Racer wheel.

The DVD wheels pictured here lack the benefit of extra traction.

DVD wheels can gain extra traction with rubber bands or balloon parts.

Clear spacers from CD or DVD spindles or DVD layers purchased at retail stores are another option for mousetrap racer wheels.

A Dremel™ tool can be used to reduce the mass, and therefore the rotational inertia, on CDs, DVDs, and DVD layers used for wheels. This makes them go faster.

Little Moe

Little Moe is probably the most basic design for a mousetrap racer, despite retaining significant versatility. It is designed for distance and speed.

The construction is simple: one end of a string is tied to the tip of a lever arm that is attached to the mousetrap's lever arm. The other end of the string has a loop designed to catch a hook attached to the drive axle.

Place the loop over the axle hook and wind the string around the drive axle by turning the wheels in the opposite direction to the racer's intended motion.

As the string winds around the axle, the lever arm is pulled closer to the drive axle, causing the mousetrap's spring to wind up and store energy. Release the drive wheels and the lever arm pulls the string off the drive axle, causing the wheels to rotate.

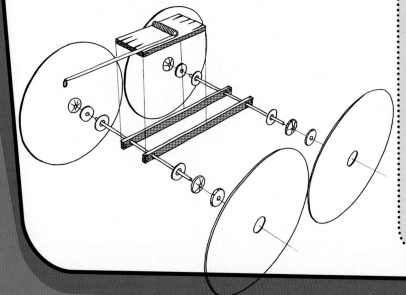

Identify and check off the following parts from the list below.

[ ] 1 - Standard Victor™ brand mousetrap

[ ] 1 - Length of Kevlar™ fishing string, such as Spider Wire™ (14 to 20 lb test)

[ ] 1 - 12" x $3/16$" brass tube (axles)

[ ] 1 - 12" x $1/8$" brass tube (lever arm)

[ ] 8 - $1/4$" L beveled faucet washers

[ ] 4 - SAE #10 flat washers

[ ] 4 - DVDs, CDs, or DVD layers

[ ] 1 - 4" zip tie

[ ] 1 - 36" x $1/2$" x $1/8$" piece of balsa wood

[ ] Ruler

[ ] Pencil

[ ] Hobby saw, such as the one offered by X-Acto™

[ ] Scrap wood or cardboard

[ ] Painters' tape or masking tape

[ ] Drill press or hand-held power drill and square

[ ] $3/8$" and $3/16$" bits for chosen drill

[ ] Cyanoacrylate glue, such as Instant Jet Glue™

[ ] Needle-nose pliers

[ ] Wire cutters

[ ] Vise

The faucet washers, available at hardware stores, fit inside the hole of either the DVDs or CDs. The other items can be found at hobby, hardware, or discount stores.

After you've followed the steps on pages 54 to 63, you will have completed your first Mousetrap Racer—the incredible Little Moe!

Little Moe—Step-by-Step

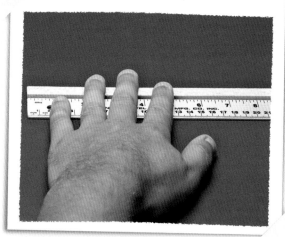

1 Measure the first side rail: it will be 8" from the 36" balsa wood strip.

2 Draw a cutting line using a straight edge at the 8" mark.

Never cut through balsa wood in a single pass. Make several light pressure cuts instead.

3 Use a hobby saw, such as the one offered by X-Acto™, and cut along the cutting line. Be sure to have a piece of scrap wood or cardboard under your balsa so you don't damage the surface underneath when cutting through the wood.

4 Use the cut side rail as a guide to make a second side rail. Put the pieces cut edge over cut edge and then cut so that your two pieces will be exactly the same length.

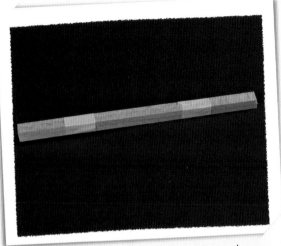

5 True up and tape the two side rails together so the pieces remain true for drilling the axle holes. Tape 1" from each end.

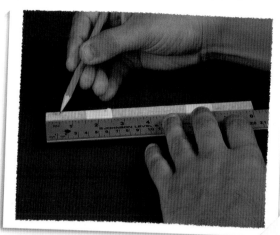

6 With the two pieces taped together, measure in $^3/_4$" from both ends and use your eye to center the marks.

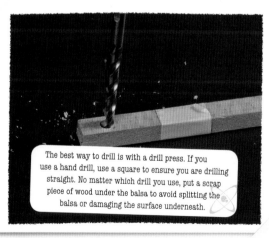

> The best way to drill is with a drill press. If you use a hand drill, use a square to ensure you are drilling straight. No matter which drill you use, put a scrap piece of wood under the balsa to avoid splitting the balsa or damaging the surface underneath.

7 Use a $^3/_8$" bit and drill the two holes.

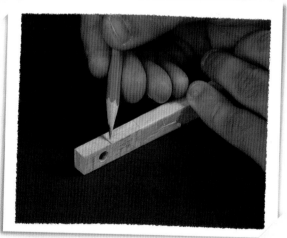

8 Before removing the tape, mark the two pieces of balsa so you know which ends were trued up. After you've made your marks, take the tape off.

Little Moe — Step-by-Step

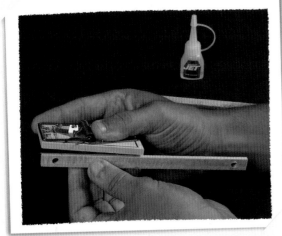

9 Attach one side rail to the bottom of the mousetrap. The front of the side rail should be flush with the front of the mousetrap.

Mark the trued-up and machine-cut edges of your balsa pieces. If you assemble it incorrectly, the axles will not line up and your racer might curve.

10 Add superglue along the joint.

The direction the mousetrap's bail points when the spring is not under tension is the front of the racer.

11 Line up the second side rail, making sure the marks on it line up with the true mark of the first side rail.

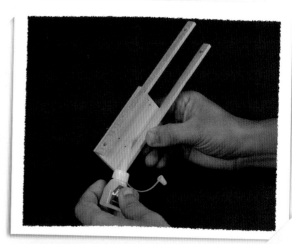

12 Holding the assembly in place, apply superglue along the joint.

Do not forget to remove the staple that holds the locking bar in place.

13 Disassemble the mousetrap using a pair of needle-nose pliers. Take off the locking bar and set it aside to be used later.

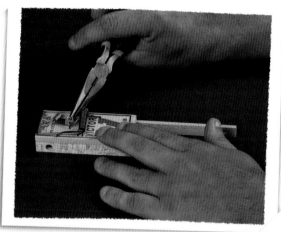

14 Remove the bait pedal. The racer will work if it is there, but removing it reduces mass and friction.

15 Raise the mousetrap's bail and use wire cutters to cut it at the corner on the side where the mousetrap's spring arm is pushing against the bail. The rest of the bail will come off. Discard it.

While cutting the brass tube, hold it steady in a vise. Do not tighten the vise too much: it will crush the tube.

16 The lever arm will be cut from a 12" x ⅛" brass tube. Cut the tube in half to make a 6" lever arm. Use a vise to hold the tube and your hobby saw to cut it.

Little Moe—Step-by-Step

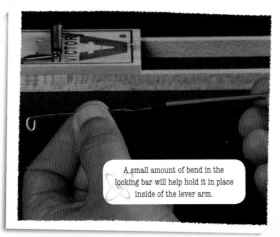

A small amount of bend in the locking bar will help hold it in place inside of the lever arm.

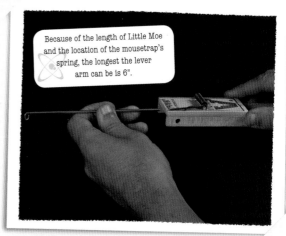

Because of the length of Little Moe and the location of the mousetrap's spring, the longest the lever arm can be is 6".

17 Using the locking bar that was set aside previously, slightly straighten the non-loop end with needle-nose pliers so it will fit snugly inside the brass tube lever arm.

18 Slide the other end of the lever arm over the cut bail arm still connected to the mousetrap, making sure the tube slides under the mousetrap's spring arm at the base of the bail.

19 Using your ruler and a pencil, mark the 12" x 3/16" brass tube at the halfway mark. Then, cut the tube, like in Step 16, to make two 6" axles.

20 Loosen or test fit the faucet washers to the axle and run them down the length of the tube. Put a penny between your thumb and the washer to avoid injury if pushing the washers on by hand, or place the washer on a hard surface and push the axle through it.

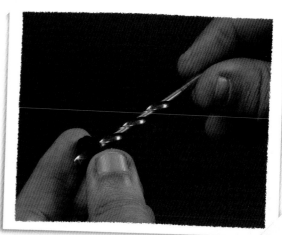

21 If you are having a hard time getting your washer on the axle, you can solve the problem by winding the washer on a ³/₁₆" drill bit by hand. Doing so will take out any burrs.

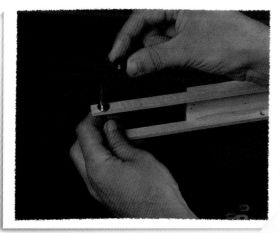

22 Slide the front and back axles into position through the axle holes. Put an SAE #10 flat washer on both sides, followed by a faucet washer, flat side in. Leave ⅛" of space between the washers and the side rails. The axle should slide back and forth.

23 Use a ruler to center the axles.

Little Moe—Step-by-Step

24 Insert faucet washers into the centers of your CD/DVD wheels.

Placing the metal washers between the wood and the faucet washer will reduce the side-to-side friction of the faucet washer rubbing against the wood frame.

25 Slide the wheels onto the axles with the flat sides of the washers pointing out.

One additional way to help reduce friction is to apply graphite to your mousetrap's spring. It can help the spring work more smoothly and improve the power applied to pulling the string.

26 The mousetrap racer has its axles, wheels, and lever in place.

27 Use the 4" zip tie to create your racer's axle hook. Tie and super-glue the zip tie to the center of the axle. Trim the extra zip tie so there is no extra tie sticking out of the zip lock.

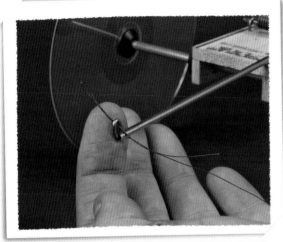

28 Using Kevlar™ string, tie a loop knot through the lever arm's locking bar loop. The type of knot you use is not important as long as it is secure.

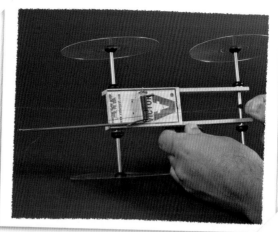

29 With the lever arm and mousetrap in the relaxed position, stretch the string from the front of the lever arm to the drive axle. Tie a loop knot so the string just barely reaches the axle hook.

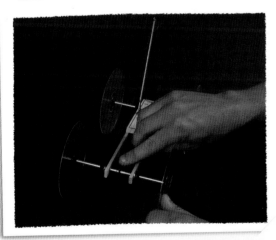

30 Gently lift the lever, attach the loop to the axle hook, and begin winding the wheel in the direction opposite to the racer's intended direction. Use a rear wheel as the winder.

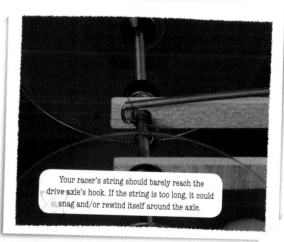

Your racer's string should barely reach the drive axle's hook. If the string is too long, it could snag and/or rewind itself around the axle.

31 After a few rotations, let go of the lever. Allow tension from winding the string around the axle to pull the lever arm toward the axle. Wind completely and your racer is ready to go.

String Theory

The moustrap racer uses string to transfer power from the spring to the drive wheels. Choosing the right string is critical. If you use a lightweight thread, it will snap under the pulling force of the mousetrap. If you use a thick string, it will not wind smoothly around the drive axle, making the pullng force inconsistent. Don't use regular nylon fishing line, because it stretches and it is difficult to knot. Use braided fishing line made of Kevlar.

Kevlar is used for bulletproof vests becuse it is strong and does not stretch. Braided Kevlar line is thin enough to wind and unwind around a small axle without tangling.

All the car designs in this book use an axle hook that catches a loop tied in the end of the string. The axle hook allows the string to slip off at the end of each run. If you tie the string to the axle, it will begin to rewind itself and stop your car. Do not tie the string to the drive axle.

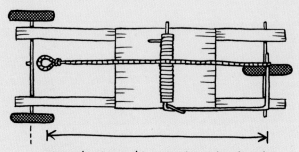

String length should be a bit shorter than the distance from the lever arm to the drive axle. This will allow the loop to release from the hook, preventing the strong from rewinding.

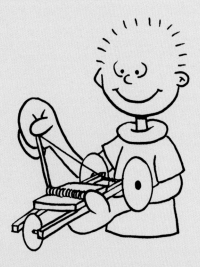

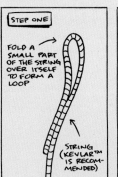

STEP ONE

FOLD A SMALL PART OF THE STRING OVER ITSELF TO FORM A LOOP

STRING (KEVLAR™ IS RECOMMENDED)

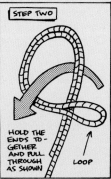

STEP TWO

HOLD THE ENDS TO-GETHER AND PULL THROUGH AS SHOWN

LOOP

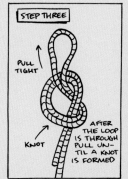

STEP THREE

PULL TIGHT

KNOT

AFTER THE LOOP IS THROUGH PULL UN-TIL A KNOT IS FORMED

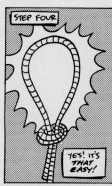

STEP FOUR

YES! IT'S *THAT* EASY!

Too much string will not wind tightly and will tangle unwinding. Use just enough string to reach the driving axle when the lever arm is in its relaxed position.

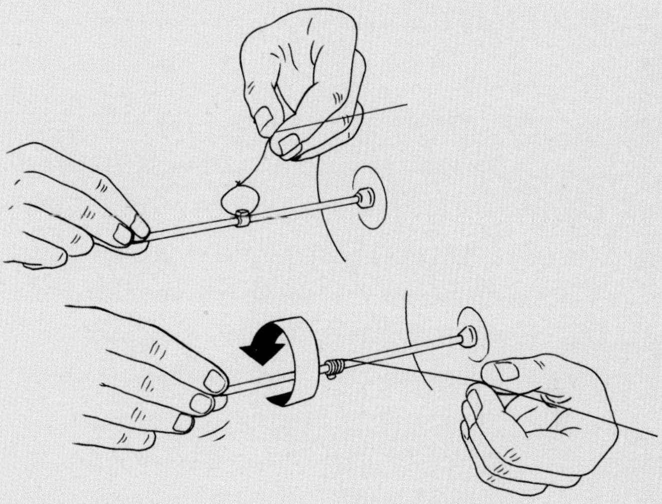

Remember, the car is going to go in the same direction as the mousetrap snaps. Roll the car in that direction on the ground and see which way the drive wheels turn. To wind the car, place the loop in the end of the string over the axle hook and turn the car's driving wheels in the OPPOSITE direction. As the string winds around the axle, it pulls the mousetrap's snapper arm down close to the drive axle. The mousetrap spring stores potential energy.

When you set the car on the floor and release the drive wheels, the mousetrap pulls the string off the drive axle and rotates the wheels, propelling the car forward.

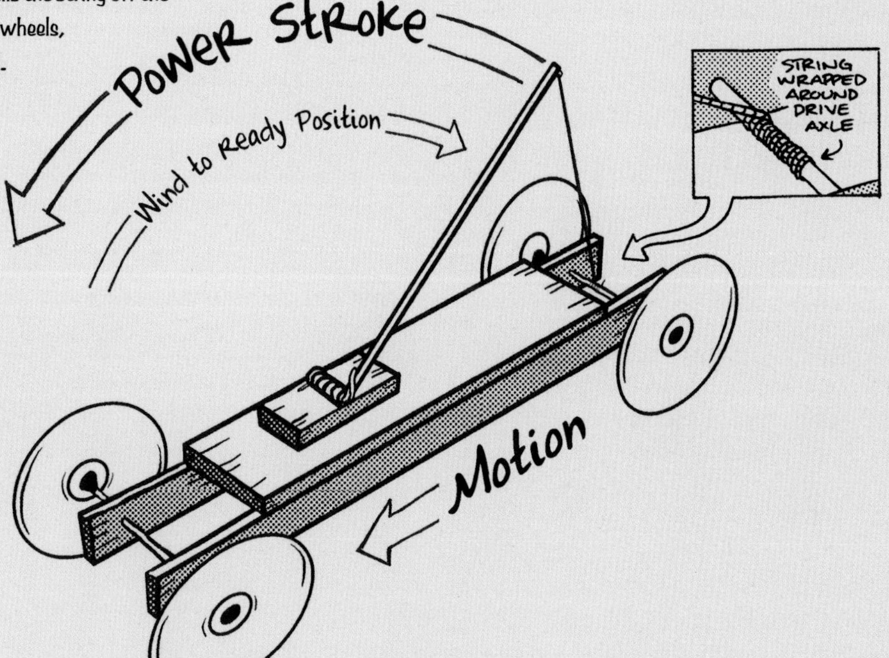

Power Stroke

Wind to Ready Position

STRING WRAPPED AROUND DRIVE AXLE

Motion

Speed-Trap

The front wheels for your Speed-Trap Racer can come from a variety of sources, such as airplane kits, other hobby shop materials, or old toys. Small slot racer wheels are another possibility. Smaller lightweight wheels have less rotational inertia and allow a Speed-Trap Racer to get to top speed quicker than larger, heavier wheels. Smaller-diameter wheels, however, create more friction over the same distance when compared to larger wheels because the smaller wheels will make more turns or rotations. Like in many other aspects of building mousetrap racers, the designer must find a balance between wheel size and travel distance.

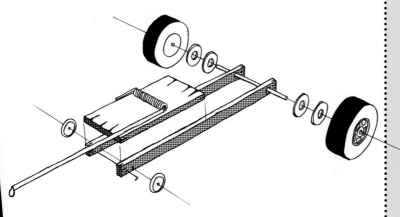

Identify and check off the following parts from the list below.

[ ] 1 - Standard Victor™ brand mousetrap

[ ] 1 - Length of Kevlar™ fishing string, such as Spider Wire™ (14 to 20 lb test)

[ ] 1 - 12" x $^5/_{32}$" brass tube (rear axle)

[ ] 1 - 12" x $^1/_8$" brass tube (lever arm)

[ ] 4 - SAE #10 flat washers

[ ] 1 - 4" zip tie

[ ] 1 - 36" x $^1/_2$" x $^1/_4$" piece of balsa wood

[ ] 1 - Set of 2" diameter rubber wheels, such as Dave Brown Lite Flight™ wheels, for rear of vehicle

[ ] 1 - Set of front wheels (plastic wheels from a balsa wood plane kit)

[ ] 1 - Piece of 3 $^1/_2$" x .032" wire (front axle)

[ ] Ruler

[ ] Pencil

[ ] Hobby saw, such as the one offered by X-Acto™

[ ] Scrap wood or cardboard

[ ] Painters' tape or masking tape

[ ] Drill press or hand-held power drill and square

[ ] $^3/_8$" bit for chosen drill

[ ] Straight edge razor, such as the hobby knife offered by X-Acto™

[ ] Cyanoacrylate glue, such as Instant Jet Glue™

[ ] Needle-nose pliers

[ ] Wire cutters

[ ] Vise

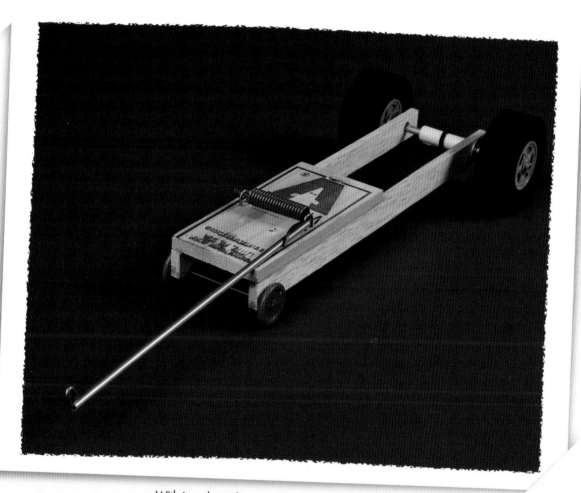

With its enlarged rear axle and small front wheels, the Speed-Trap Racer you're about to build will get you there faster than you ever thought possible!

Speed-Trap Racer—Step-by-Step

To start, go back and repeat Steps 1–7 for Little Moe. However, modify Steps 6 and 7 by marking and drilling only one set of axle holes; the front axle will be placed in a groove that you will create in Step 9. When finished, return here and continue.

8 On your two taped pieces of balsa wood, mark ½" in from the front edge.

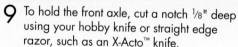

If you are using an airplane kit to provide wheels for your Speed-Trap Racer, the wire in the airplane kit will work perfectly as a front axle.

9 To hold the front axle, cut a notch ⅛" deep using your hobby knife or straight edge razor, such as an X-Acto™ knife.

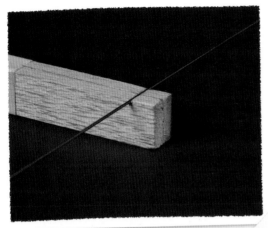

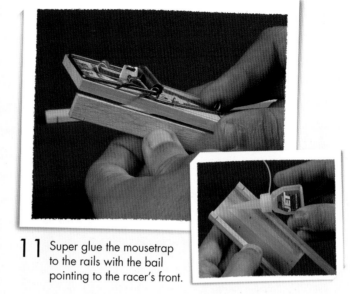

10 Test fit the front axle groove by pressing the wire axle into the groove. Remove the tape, but be sure that your axle holes and grooves have been created first.

11 Super glue the mousetrap to the rails with the bail pointing to the racer's front.

12 Return to Little Moe Steps 13 through 18 on pages 57 and 58 for instructions on how to dismantle the mousetrap and construct your lever. After completing the steps, return here.

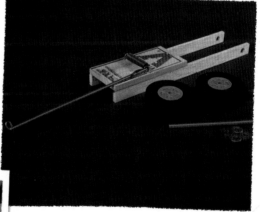

19 Cut a 3½" rear axle from the 12" x 5/32" tube and then insert it onto one of the 2" diameter rubber wheels. Attach the wheel to the axle with superglue.

Speed Trap Racer—Step-by-Step

20 Place one SAE #10 flat washer over the rear axle hole on one of the side rails. Center it and glue it in place. Glue around the washer's outside. Repeat on opposite rail.

The metal washer will keep the bronze axle from rubbing on the wooden rails, creating metal-on-metal friction, which is lower and results in less energy loss than metal-on-wood friction.

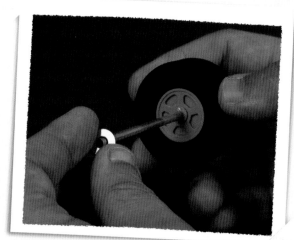

21 Slide one SAE #10 flat washer down the axle. The washer next to the plastic wheel creates metal-on-metal friction and keeps the rubber wheel from rubbing on the side rail. Use another washer if the tire rubs against the side rail.

22 Insert the axle/wheel assembly through the rear axle holes. Place your final SAE #10 flat washer on the exposed axle.

If you glue your second tire from the inside of the tire, your two washers could mistakenly end up glued together.

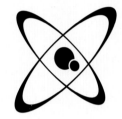

23 Place the second tire on the end of the exposed axle and glue in place. Glue from the outside of the tire.

Masking tape adds circumference to the rear axle, which yields more torque. Adding torque will result in faster speeds over a shorter distance. The number of rotations of tape around the axle is guesswork. Though you can gain speed by adding more tape, at some point, your racer will begin to spin at the start. Find the balance: How much tape can you add before performance suffers?

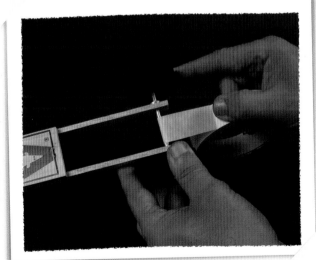

24 In order to increase torque, make 15 to 25 wraps around the center of the axle with masking tape.

Speed Trap Racer—Step-by-Step

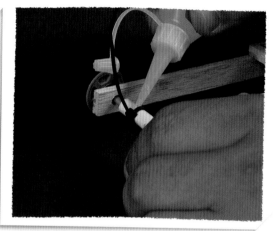

25 After adding the tape, use a zip tie to create your hook. Center the tie on the masking tape. Glue the tie in place and then trim to no more than ⅛" long.

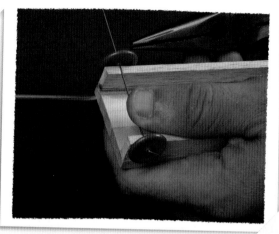

26 Use the needle-nose pliers to bend a ¼" wheel stop at the end of the 3½" x .032" wire. Put both front wheels on the wire and put the axle in the notches.

27 Determine where to bend the other wheel stop. There should be ⅛" of play for each wheel. Bend the second wheel stop and cut off the extra wire.

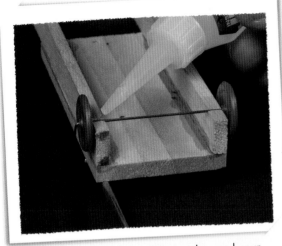

28 Glue the wire axle into the notches and your front axle assembly is complete.

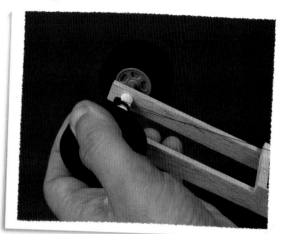

29 Tie a slipknot to the wire loop at the end of the lever. Measure just enough string to reach back to the hook. Tie a loop at the end of the string. Raise the lever arm enough to allow you to hook the loop and begin winding.

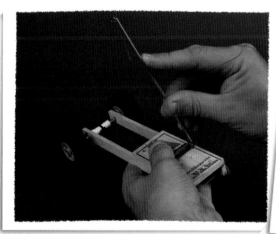

30 Bend the lever over to the center of the racer slightly. The lever should pull through the centerline of the racer.

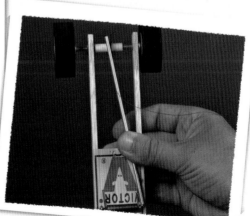

Improving speed racers

If your mousetrap racer does not seem to move with enough speed, here are some ideas to try.

- Apply graphite powder between the wheels, the flat washers, and the frame to reduce friction.
- Shorter lever arms have more pulling force. More pulling force means greater acceleration. Greater acceleration means less time before the racer reaches top speed. If the lever arm is too short, your racer will slip off the start and waste energy. Adjust the lever length in order to find the best performance.
- Wheels should be around 2" to 5" in diameter but no larger than a compact disc. If the wheel-to-axle ratio is too small, your racer will slip off the start and will waste energy. Therefore, adjust the ratio in order to find the best performance.
- If your racer spins at the start, increase the traction. Use rubber bands or stretched balloon parts on the drive wheels to increase the traction. Athletic sneaker sole treatments, such as B-Sharp Traction Action™, will also help the wheels gain traction. More traction means greater acceleration.
- You can get more torque with a thick axle. More torque means greater acceleration. You can build the axle up with tape to increase the axle diameter.

- Design the racer to have a large power output in a short period. With a speed racer, the objective is to quickly convert potential into kinetic energy.
- Use lightweight wheels. A wheel with large rotational inertia can really limit a racer's performance. Using a rotary carving tool, like a Dremel, remove as much mass as possible from the wheels.
- Is the problem the mousetrap? Not all springs have the same spring tension. The greater the tension, the more energy will be stored when the spring is wound up.

Super speed secrets from Doc Fizzix

To increase your speed further, try:

■ Moving the mousetrap closer to the drive axle and decreasing the length of the lever arm accordingly.

■ Increasing traction by adding mass directly above the drive axle.

■ Moving the mousetrap away from drive wheel(s) only if the wheels are slipping. The move will decrease the pulling force that is the reason for the slipping wheels.

■ Decreasing rolling friction by reworking friction points. Polish bushings (see page 94) or use ball bearings. If you are using bearings, soak them in WD-40™. Soaking will help remove oil or grease (see page 94). Although grease and oil are lubricants and often used to reduce friction, adding them to mousetrap racer bearings slows the racer down because of the large viscosities of the lubricants.

■ Adjusting the wheel-to-axle ratio by adding or removing tape on the drive axle.

■ Checking string alignment and making sure the string is attached directly over the drive axle with the lever arm held in the fully wound position.

■ Using smaller-diameter wheels.

Basic Racer I

The Basic Racer I is a great all-around racer. It can go fast. It can travel long distances. It can carry weight. With some modifications, it can specialize in any of those functions. Follow these steps and tips to create your own version of the racer.

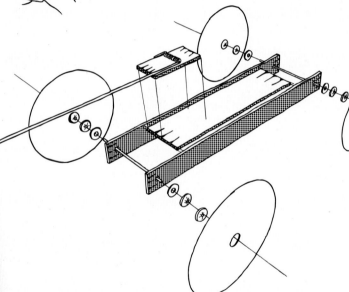

Identify and check off the following parts from the list below.

[] 1 - Standard Victor™ brand mousetrap

[] 1 - Length of Kevlar™ fishing string, such as Spider Wire™ (14 to 20 lb test)

[] 1 - 12" x ³/₁₆" brass tube (axles)

[] 1 - 12" x ⅛" brass tube

[] 8 - ¼" L beveled faucet washers

[] 4 - SAE #10 flat washers

[] 4 - DVDs, CDs, or DVD halves (wheels)

[] 1 - 4" zip tie

[] 1 - 36" x 3" x ⅛" or ³/₁₆" piece of balsa wood

[] Metal ruler

[] Pencil

[] Straight edge razor or hobby knife, such as an X-Acto™ knife

[] Scrap wood or cardboard

[] Masking or painters' tape

[] Drill press or hand-held power drill and square

[] ³/₈" bit for chosen drill

[] Cyanoacrylate glue, such as Instant Jet Glue™

[] Vise

[] Hobby saw, such as the one offered by X-Acto™

[] Needle-nose pliers

[] Wire cutters

[] Graphite

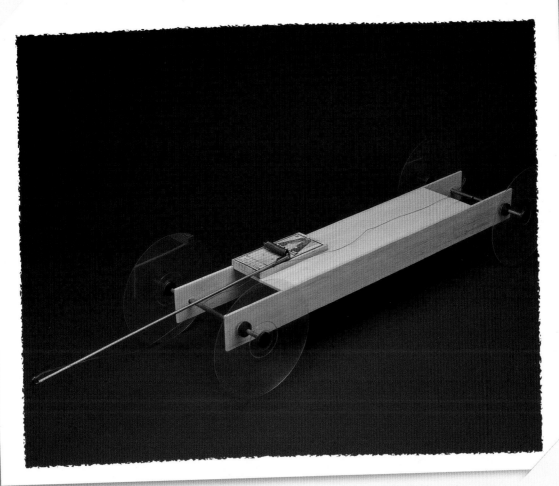

The amazing Basic Racer I can be either a great racer on its own or can be the starting point for a series of special Doc Fizzix features!

Basic Racer 1—Step-by-Step

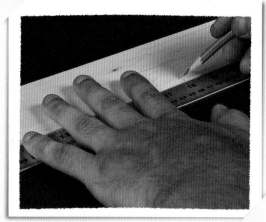

1 From the 36" x 3" piece of balsa, cut two 18" x 3" pieces with your straight edge razor or hobby knife. Remember to use many light cuts to avoid splintering your balsa; cut only a few fibers at a time. Be sure to protect your cutting surface with a piece of scrap wood or cardboard under your balsa.

2 Cut 6" of length from one of the 18" x 3" cut pieces of balsa, making one piece that is 12" x 3". This will be your deck top.

3 Cut the 18" x 3" piece of balsa in half lengthwise to make two pieces measuring 18 x 1½". Mark the piece at the halfway point on the 3" ends and use your ruler as a straight edge between the two marks. Cut with your straight edge razor or hobby knife.

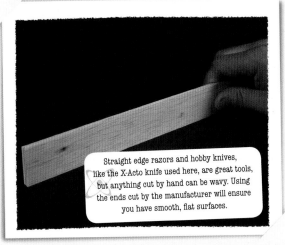

Straight edge razors and hobby knives, like the X-Acto knife used here, are great tools, but anything cut by hand can be wavy. Using the ends cut by the manufacturer will ensure you have smooth, flat surfaces.

4 To make the side rails, stack the two 18" x 1½" pieces of cut balsa, lining up one of the short ends. It is best to line up the manufacturer-cut ends as much as possible.

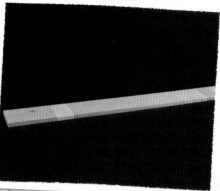

5 After you've lined up the edges cut by the manufacturer, tape around the two 18" x 1½" pieces approximately 4" from each end. Make a mark across the top of the two pieces so you know how they were lined up during the drilling.

6 Working from each end, measure ¾" in from the front of the side rail and make a mark that crosses from top to bottom. Make another line that runs through the center of the side rails and the first line. At the intersection of the two lines, poke the balsa with a pencil to give the drill a starting point.

7 Using either a drill press or a hand-held power drill, use a ⅜" bit to drill the two holes. Remember to put scrap wood under the balsa while drilling.

Basic Racer I—Step-by-Step

8 Measure in 3" on the top of your two rails (the manufactured edges) and make a mark. You should see your original mark that shows how the pieces were lined up when the holes were drilled.

9 Place the corner of the 12" x 3" deck top at the 3" mark on one side rail and hold the pieces together. Hold the deck top flush with the top true edge of the side rail.

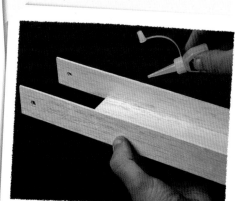

10 While holding the two pieces together, turn them over and glue in place using cyanoacrylate glue, such as Instant Jet Glue™. Attach the other side rail in the same way.

11 Use a vise and your hobby saw to cut two 6" x $^3/_{16}$" brass tubes from the 12" x $^3/_{16}$" tube. Be sure not to crush the tube in the vise! The 6" tubes will be your racer's axles.

12 Slide the front axle into position through the axle holes. Put an SAE #10 flat washer on both sides, followed by a faucet washer, flat side in. Leave $^1/_8$" of space between the washers and the side rails. The axle should slide back and forth and the washers should not be tight on against the frame. Repeat the process for the back axle.

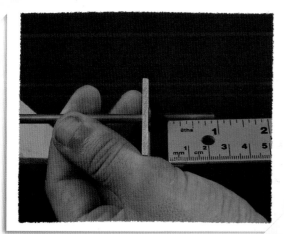

13 Center the axle between the side rails by adjusting the rubber faucet washers. There should be about $^1/_8$" to $^1/_4$" side-to-side play along the axle.

Basic Racer I—Step-by-Step

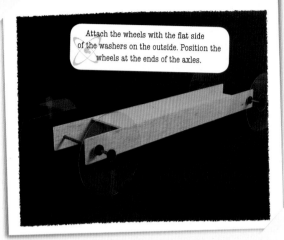

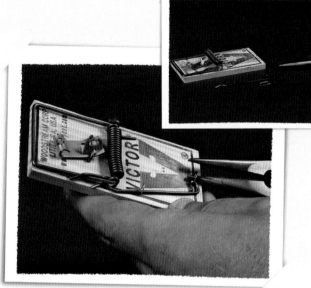

Attach the wheels with the flat side of the washers on the outside. Position the wheels at the ends of the axles.

14 Insert faucet washers into the centers of your CD/DVD wheels. Push the wheels onto the axles.

15 Use needle-nose pliers to remove the mousetrap's locking bar and the staple that holds it in place. Save the locking bar for later use with the lever arm.

16 Remove the bait pad. Again, as with Little Moe and Speed-Trap Racer, you do not have to remove it, but it does add mass and therefore will increase friction, slowing your racer.

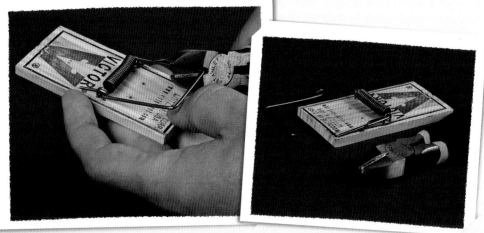

17 Raise the mousetrap's bail and use wire cutters to cut it at the corner on the side where the mousetrap's spring arm is pushing against it. The rest of the bail will come off. Discard it.

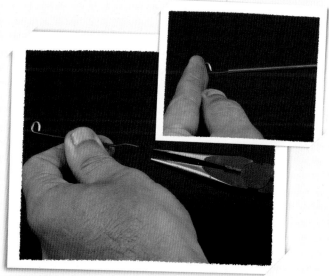

18 Use needle-nose pliers to slightly straighten the locking bar you removed earlier. Insert the locking bar into the 12" x ⅛" brass tube. The locking bar should fit snugly into the tube. The lever is now complete.

The direction the bail points when the mousetrap's spring is not under tension determines the front of the mousetrap and racer.

19 Slide the other end of the lever over the mousetrap's cut bail, making sure the tube slides under the mousetrap's spring arm at the base of the bail.

Basic Racer I—Step-by-Step

20 On top of the deck top (the side that's level with the side rail edges), position the back end of the mousetrap $10\frac{1}{4}$" from the drive axle. The mousetrap should be positioned so the lever arm points toward the front of the racer and travels along the center axis of the racer.

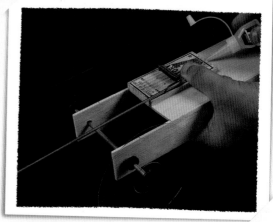

21 Double-check to ensure the lever arm does not extend beyond the rear axle, and then glue the mousetrap in place with cyanoacrylate.

22 Attach the zip tie around the center of the rear axle to create the axle hook. Trim the tie so no more than $\frac{1}{8}$" remains above the zip lock. Use superglue to fix your hook to the axle.

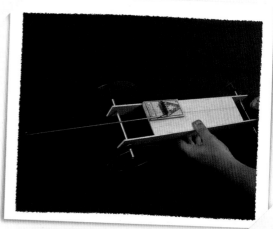

23 Tie one end of the Kevlar string to the locking bar loop on the tip of the lever arm. Tie a loop knot on the free end of the string so it is just long enough to reach to the axle hook when the lever is relaxed. Cut off any extra string.

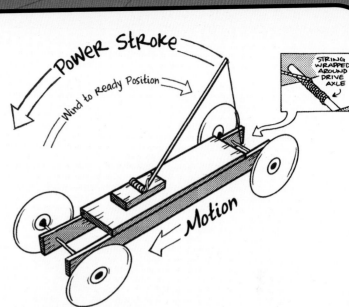

Power Stroke

Wind to Ready Position

STRING WRAPPED AROUND DRIVE AXLE

Motion

24 Hook the loop knot over the axle hook and lift the lever a bit to start winding the string in the direction opposite to the direction in which you want the racer to travel. After a couple of turns, release the lever and keep winding the string tightly.

25 Before racing your car, be sure to apply graphite on the washers and mousetrap spring—any place you believe friction could occur. Any amount of friction you eliminate will make your racer run better.

Basic Racer II

The Basic Racer II combines the best elements of Basic Racer I and the opportunity to try a variety of advanced techniques—see Chapter 4, beginning on page 92. Its best feature is its versatility.

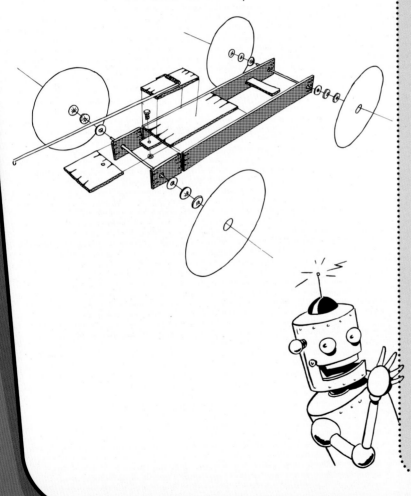

Identify and check off the following parts from the list below.

[] 1 - Standard Victor™ brand mousetrap

[] 1 - Length of Kevlar™ fishing string, such as Spider Wire™ (14 to 20 lb test)

[] 1 - 12" x 3/16" brass tube (axles)

[] 1 - 12" x 1/8" brass tube (lever arm)

[] 8 - 1/4" L beveled faucet washers

[] 4 - SAE #10 flat washers

[] 1 - 1/4-20 x 3/4" plastic bolt and nut

[] 4 - DVDs, CDs, or DVD halves (wheels)

[] 1 - 4" zip tie

[] 1 - 36" x 3" x 1/8" or 3/16" piece of balsa wood

[] Square

[] Straight edge razor or hobby knife, such as an X-Acto™ knife

[] Scrap wood or cardboard

[] Metal ruler

[] Masking or painters' tape

[] Pencil

[] Drill press or hand-held power drill

[] 3/8" bit for chosen drill

[] Cyanoacrylate glue, such as Instant Jet Glue™

[] Vise

[] Hobby saw, such as the one offered by X-Acto™

[] Needle-nose pliers

[] Wire cutters

[] Graphite

Ready to build a racer that can steer itself? Try the Basic Racer II—a great car for racing or the starting point for many specialized Doc Fizzix cars.

Basic Racer II—Step-by-Step

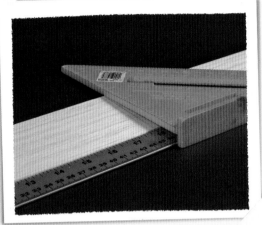

1 Mark the 36" x 3" piece of balsa wood at 18" x 3". Use a square to ensure the line is accurate. Using a metal ruler and a straight edge razor or hobby knife, like an X-Acto™ knife, cut your piece of balsa wood in half to create two 18" x 3" pieces.

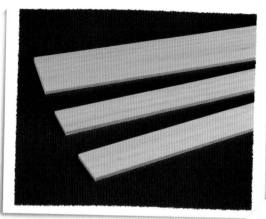

2 Mark one 18" x 3" piece at the halfway point on each 3" end and use your metal ruler as a straightedge between the two marks. Cut the piece into two 18" x 1½" pieces with your straight edge razor.

3 Line up the manufacturer-cut edges of the two 18" x 1½" balsa pieces. Tape around the stack approximately 4" from each end. Make a mark across the thin sides of the balsa pieces so you know how they were stacked.

4 Working from the manufacturer-cut end and side of the taped stack, measure and make two intersecting lines ¾" in from the end and from the side. At the intersection of the two lines, poke the balsa with a pencil to give the drill a starting point. Repeat on the other end of the stack.

5 Use a drill press or hand-held power drill with a square, along with the appropriate $3/8$" drill bit, to drill a hole through the side rails at both pencil marks.

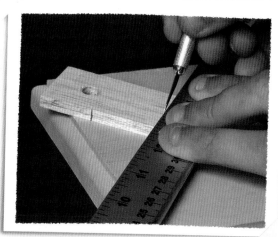

6 Using a straight edge and razor blade, cut off a $2\frac{1}{2}$" piece from each side rail. These pieces will be the front side rails of the steering assembly, while the leftover $15\frac{1}{2}$" x $1\frac{1}{2}$" pieces will be the rear side rails.

7 Using the remaining 18" x 3" piece, measure and cut a $2\frac{1}{2}$" x 3" piece. This will be part of the steering assembly.

Basic Racer II—Step-by-Step

8 Using the leftover 15½" x 3" piece, measure and cut a 7" x 3" piece. This will be the deck top. When you have completed the cut, you should have the configuration at far right.

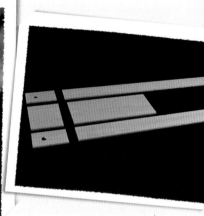

9 Using the remaining 8½" x 3" piece of balsa wood, measure and cut two 1" x 3" pieces. One of these will be the flange in the steering assembly; one will act as a stabilizer.

10 Take one of the 1" x 3" pieces; mark ½" in on a 1" side and draw a line through the center as shown. Take the 2½" x 3" piece, mark the piece at ½", and then draw a line through the center. With a drill press or hand-held power drill, use a ¼" bit to drill holes through both pieces where the lines intersect. These are the flange and the center of the steering assembly.

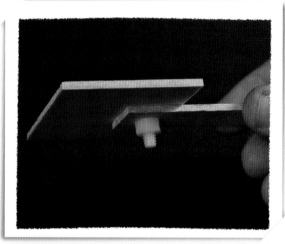

11 Use your ¼-20 x ¾" plastic bolt and nut to connect the 1" x 3" and 2½" x 3" pieces as shown to begin your steering assembly.

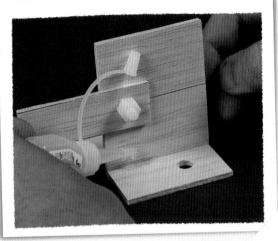

12 Super-glue one 2½" x 1½" front side rail to the steering assembly by placing the axle hole on the edge furthest away from the nut and bolt as shown.

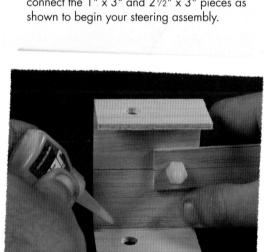

13 Super-glue the second 2½" x 1½" front side rail as in Step 12. Your steering assembly is now complete.

14 Attach one 15½" x 1½" rear side rail to the 7" x 3" deck top with cyanoacrylate glue; line up the non-drilled end of the side rail with the front edge of the deck top. Super-glue along the inside corner. Attach the second rear side rail in the same way.

Basic Racer II—Step-by-Step

15 Position the remaining 1" x 3" piece of balsa 3" from the rear of the frame and glue it into place as shown above. The balsa piece will act as a stabilizer to keep the frame from flexing. The chassis—deck top, rear side rails, and stabilizer—is now complete.

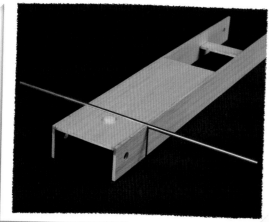

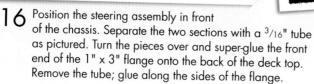

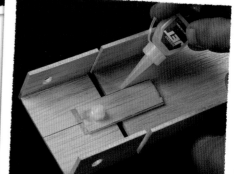

16 Position the steering assembly in front of the chassis. Separate the two sections with a 3/16" tube as pictured. Turn the pieces over and super-glue the front end of the 1" x 3" flange onto the back of the deck top. Remove the tube; glue along the sides of the flange.

The steering mechanism can become invaluable if the surface upon which you are racing is not perfectly flat and requires you to steer right or left to keep your racer straight. Learn to "play the curve."

17 Adjust the plastic nut and bolt enough that the front section will still swivel with a little pressure. Adjust the position of the steering assembly before winding and releasing the racer to control the steering.

18 Basic Racer II can be completed by following Steps 11 through 25 for Basic Racer I on pages 79 to 83. Note: As you proceed with some of the more advanced racer techniques available through Basic Racer II, you may decide it is worth installing ball bearings (visit Chapter 4).

CHAPTER 4

Advanced Models and Construction Techniques

For some types of competitions, different construction or preparation techniques are required. The world of physics allows you to take the concept of mousetrap racers from a fairly basic level into considerably more advanced areas that require greater understanding of construction techniques and science. Would you like to power your racer with the least amount of surface friction possible? Want to build a boomerang racer that goes forward and then stops and returns to you? How about a twin-engine racer powered by two mousetraps? Maybe a long lever designed for extra distance is what you need. Serious builders might consider adding ball bearings to their racer, while determined distance competitors might opt to develop their own Big Wheel car. You'll find it all here in the *Advanced Models and Construction Techniques* chapter.

Ball bearings

Minimizing surface friction on a mousetrap racer allows its wheels to spin with less resistance, taking it faster and farther with less energy waste. The most common area where surface friction will occur is between the axle and the chassis. If your plan is to create a racer that will go the fastest or farthest, ball bearings are one option to consider.

A bearing is the interface between the axle and the chassis; this can be as simple as an axle turning in a drilled hole. A bushing is a smooth sleeve placed in a hole that gives the axle a smoother rubbing surface, which means less friction.

Ball bearings are made up of small roller balls inside a two-piece casing. As an axle turns, the roller balls turn and provide a very smooth, reduced-friction surface. A rolling ball has little friction and ball bearings usually provide the best performance.

Bearings manufactured to a $3/16$" inner diameter may not fit an axle with the same $3/16$" outer diameter. Bearings are manufactured to much higher standards than axles. A bearing may fit one brass tube but not another. Do not force bearings onto an axle; the force could destroy the bearing.

How to install bearings

1 To remove the pre-packed grease from a bearing, soak it in WD-40™ for several minutes.

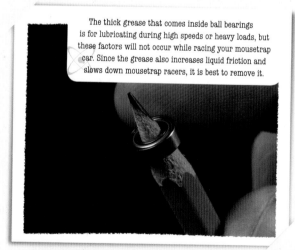

The thick grease that comes inside ball bearings is for lubricating during high speeds or heavy loads, but these factors will not occur while racing your mousetrap car. Since the grease also increases liquid friction and slows down mousetrap racers, it is best to remove it.

2 Remove the bearing from the solvent and put it on the tip of a pencil. Spin the bearing to sling the grease from the bearing. Continue until all of the grease has been removed.

3 Hobby stores that sell radio-controlled cars usually sell bearings, but not all bearings will fit on a $^3/_{16}$" brass tube. You may find the tube and bearing are a very tight fit.

4 If the axle won't fit into the bearing, the best solution is to insert the tube into your power drill and use 320- to 400-grit wet sandpaper to reduce the diameter of the tube. Turn the drill on to a low speed, hold the sandpaper around the axle, and move it along the length of the tubing.

5 When the ball bearings fit on the axle, insert them into the holes drilled for the axle. When installing ball bearings in a mousetrap racer, drill axle holes in your balsa wood using a drill bit slightly smaller than the outer diameter of the bearings. Balsa has a bit of flex to it, so the bearing should fit snugly. Slide the axle into place. Repeat for the back axle.

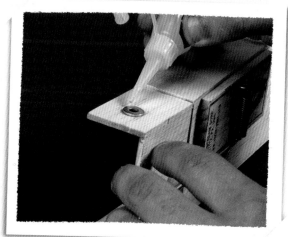

6 If you are not using ball bearings, use SAE #10 washers to help reduce the bearing friction. Glue the washer to the outside of the axle hole and allow the axle to ride on the metal washer.

The perfect distance car

A good distance traveler will move slowly, wasting as little energy as possible with air resistance. As you design your racer, remember that good aerodynamics will improve the performance of any racer.

Sand your racer smooth, leaving few points for air drag. Inspect the body for flat surfaces on leading edges that could catch air, thus increasing the air drag. Rounding the leading edges of your racer will allow for smoother movement of air around your racer. Tires should be thin because thin tires are more aerodynamic and will slice through the air more smoothly. Wider tires have more air drag.

Doc Fizzix's super-secret tips for improving distance racers:

■ **Longer lever arms**

More string pulled off the drive axle translates into more turns of the wheels: the racer will cover more distance under the same pulling force.

■ **Large drive wheel(s)**

Large drive wheels cover more linear distance for each rotation. The best distance wheels tend to be between 1' and 2' in diameter.

■ **Small drive axle**

A smaller axle turns more for the same length of string than a larger one. More axle rotations mean more turns of the wheel and greater travel distance.

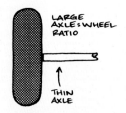

LARGE AXLE:WHEEL RATIO

THIN AXLE

Use a large wheel-to-axle ratio with distance vehicles.

■ **Small power output**

Slower racers are more energy efficient. Slow a racer down by increasing the lever arm length and repositioning the mousetrap further from the drive axle. At low speeds, air resistance is not a large factor in the motion of a moving object and more energy goes to linear distance.

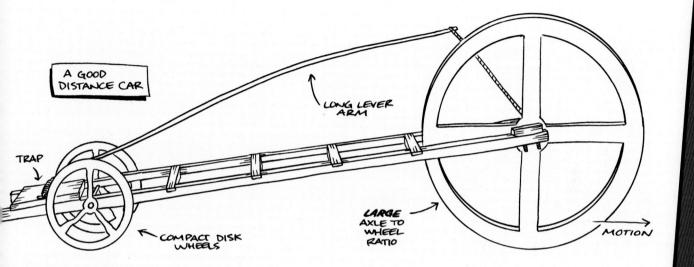

A GOOD DISTANCE CAR

TRAP

LONG LEVER ARM

COMPACT DISK WHEELS

LARGE AXLE TO WHEEL RATIO

MOTION

■ Remove ALL friction

An impossible goal, but the more you can reduce friction, the less energy will be lost to heat and sound, which translates into greater speed. Your racer should have the lowest possible energy consumption due to friction.

■ Decrease rolling friction

Polish bushings or use ball bearings. If you are using bearings, soak them in WD-40 to remove any oil or grease. Although grease and oil are lubricants and often used to reduce friction, adding the thick substances to mousetrap racer bearings increases liquid friction and slows the racer. Find more information about ball bearings on page 94.

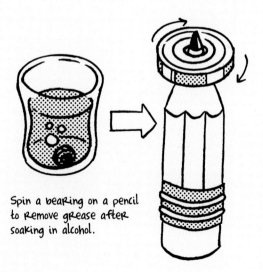

Spin a bearing on a pencil to remove grease after soaking in alcohol.

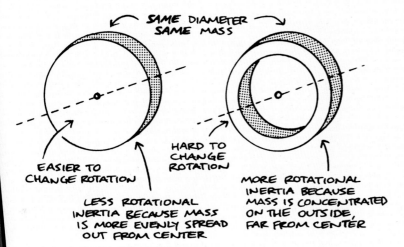

SAME DIAMETER
SAME MASS

EASIER TO
CHANGE ROTATION

HARD TO
CHANGE
ROTATION

LESS ROTATIONAL
INERTIA BECAUSE MASS
IS MORE EVENLY SPREAD
OUT FROM CENTER

MORE ROTATIONAL
INERTIA BECAUSE
MASS IS CONCENTRATED
ON THE OUTSIDE,
FAR FROM CENTER

■ **Decrease mass and rotational inertia**

Build a lightweight frame and use lightweight wheels. Remove mass from wheels to decrease rotational inertia. If possible, avoid adding mass, such as rubber bands or balloons, around the outside of wheels.

■ **Sample different mousetraps**

Not all mousetrap springs have exactly the same spring tension. The greater the tension, the more energy will be stored when the spring is wound.

■ **Expand the drive wheel**

Build a Big Wheel Racer using the instructions on page 100. Try making the wheel out of mat or foam board. Both are stiff and lightweight.

■ **Use a smaller drive axle**

The larger the ratio of drive wheel(s)-to-axle(s) diameter, the farther your racer will go each turn of the wheel and the greater the pulling distance will be.

■ **Check string alignment**

Make sure that the string is wound evenly around the drive axle with the lever arm held in the fully wound position.

■ **Use a rear brace**

When building your distance racer, avoid running the deck the full length of the racer. You will reduce weight and friction, save energy, and allow for faster or longer performance.

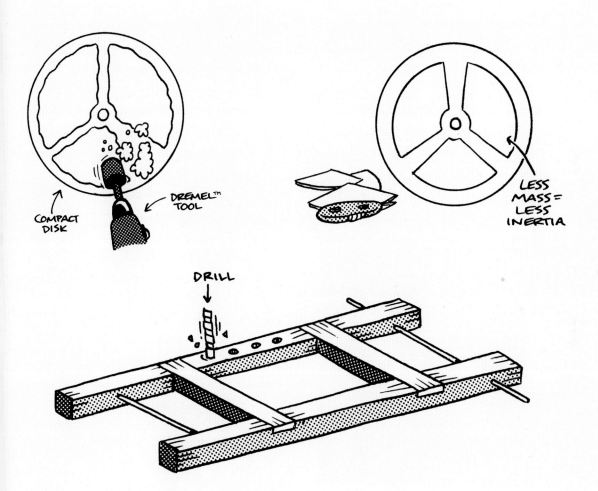

COMPACT
DISK

DREMEL™
TOOL

LESS
MASS =
LESS
INERTIA

DRILL

Methods of Reducing mass.

Big Wheel Racer

What will go farther—a Basic Racer II or a Big Wheel Racer? The answer is up to you to determine based on experimentation and documentation.

With distance racers, you want the smallest possible force acting over the longest possible distance—a racer with a large wheel-to-axle ratio. A racer with a small axle and a large wheel will cover more distance per turn of the axle compared to a smaller wheel size with the same axle.

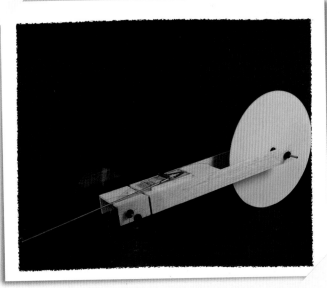

The wheel's diameter impacts how far the racer travels per axle rotation. Large-diameter wheels will make fewer turns to cover the same distance. The difference reduces the total amount of energy needed to overcome friction. For smaller-diameter wheels, less friction is applied over a smaller axle turning distance and less energy is wasted. That leaves more energy to move the racer.

The Big Wheel Racer has the advantage of traveling a greater distance for each rotation of the wheel compared to the Basic II, but the Basic II can use momentum to coast further than the Big Wheel. The Basic II is easer to build, more stable, and easier to operate, with little testing and tweaking needed to get good results. The Basic Racer II can travel more than 75 m (about 250 ft), but the average result is about 40 to 50 m (130 to 165 ft). If built correctly, the Big Wheel Racer should be the winner, but it is harder to build and takes a lot more time and fine-tuning to maximize its distance.

You will have to experiment yourself to determine what racer travels faster for you and what you can do to maximize distance.

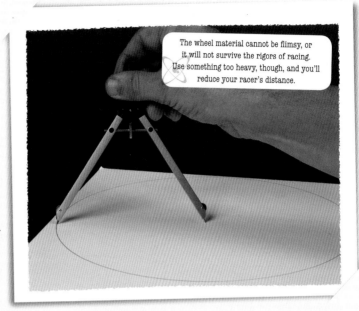

The wheel material cannot be flimsy, or it will not survive the rigors of racing. Use something too heavy, though, and you'll reduce your racer's distance.

1 Using a protractor, draw an 11"-diameter circle on mat, illustration, or foam board, or whatever material you plan to use for your Big Wheel Racer.

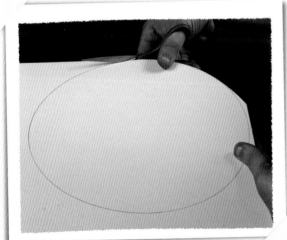

2 The illustration board used here cuts easily with a pair of scissors. Depending on the material, other tools may be necessary, such as a straight edge razor (like an X-Acto™) or scroll saw.

3 Drill a hole in the center of the wheel to match the axle you are using. If you are using a $^3/_{16}$" axle, drill the hole with a $^3/_{16}$" bit.

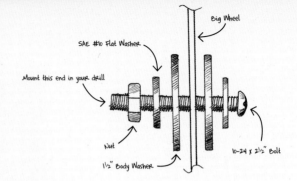

Big Wheel

SAE #10 Flat Washer

Mount this end in your drill

Nut

1½" Body Washer

10-24 x 2½" Bolt

4 Depending on your cutting abilities, it's possible your wheel will need to be rounded off in a few spots. The best way to ensure a perfect circle is to fasten the wheel to a power drill and spin the wheel against a sanding block equipped with 100-grit sandpaper. To prepare your Big Wheel for turning, use a 10-24 bolt equipped with a washer assembly as shown above. Insert the end of the bolt into the drill.

5 While sanding, maintain the distance between the block and wheel and gradually tighten it until the wheel is a perfect circle. For safety, it may be best for a second person to hold the sanding block in place.

6 When the wheel is sanded, place the axle through the center of the wheel. Press one faucet washer against each side of the wheel, flat side toward the wheel, to keep it perpendicular to the axle.

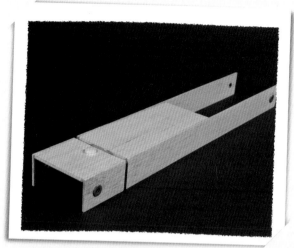

7 The Big Wheel axle assembly is used in concert with the completed Basic Racer II body. Build the Basic Racer II now, using the instructions beginning on page 84, if you haven't already. Leave off the front wheels.

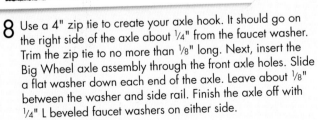

8 Use a 4" zip tie to create your axle hook. It should go on the right side of the axle about ¼" from the faucet washer. Trim the zip tie to no more than ⅛" long. Next, insert the Big Wheel axle assembly through the front axle holes. Slide a flat washer down each end of the axle. Leave about ⅛" between the washer and side rail. Finish the axle off with ¼" L beveled faucet washers on either side.

9 Attach the Kevlar™ string to the lever arm and the axle hook.

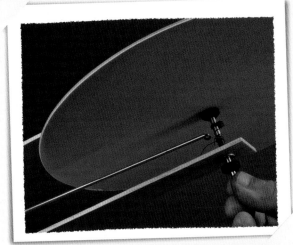

10 Wind the string completely by turning the axle in the direction opposite to the direction you want the vehicle to travel.

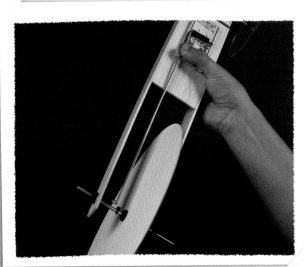

11 The string is wound completely, and with the lever held in place, the Big Wheel Racer is ready to go.

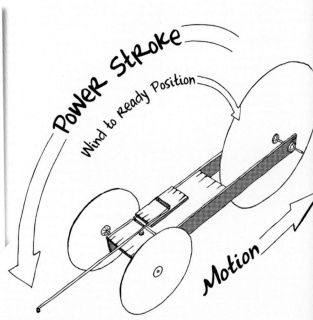

Power Stroke

Wind to Ready Position

Motion

The movable mousetrap

If you are interested in experimenting with the impact of mousetrap location on your racer, it is possible to create a racer with parts you can relocate.

1 To begin, construct any car except Little Moe or Speed-Trap Racer, but do not glue the mousetrap to the top of the racer. Instead, drill holes in the four corners of your mousetrap using a bit that matches your bolt's diameter. Use a drill press or a hand-held power drill with a square.

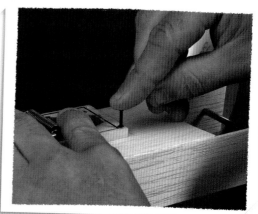

2 You can position the mousetrap in several different places on the racer's deck top: wherever you want! At each position, mark the holes on the deck top by pushing a screw through each of the four holes in the mousetrap. Remove the trap. Enhance the screw marks with a pencil.

3 Drill the anchoring holes in the deck top using a drill bit that matches the diameter of the bolts. To test the effect different mousetrap locations have on your racer, attach the mousetrap to different spots using 4-40 ½" socket head screws and blind nuts.

A longer lever

Longer lever arms tend to bend. Bending will prevent the mousetrap's spring from being fully compressed or wound-up. Using a brass brazing or steel rod or tube is a possibility for a long lever arm, but a better solution is making a lightweight lever from balsa wood.

A wooden lever arm will be stronger and lighter than any brass or steel rod or tube that you could use. The strength of the wooden arm comes from its construction: two lightweight strips of balsa wood glued together to form a T-beam. A T-beam is much lighter and in some cases more resistant to breaking under a load than a solid piece of wood or steel. Note: a T-beam can be constructed for any car except Little Moe or Speed-Trap Racer.

1 To construct a T-beam, you'll need two $1/2" \times 1/8" \times 18"$ pieces of balsa wood, one standard Victor™ brand mousetrap, and one $12" \times 3/16"$ brass tube.

2 Place one piece of balsa on top of the other, centering it along the bottom piece of wood. Use an X-Acto™ hobby saw and cut along the cutting line

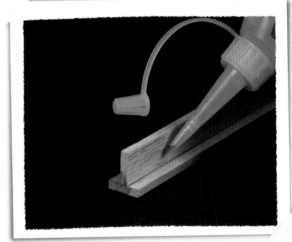

3 Glue along the seams of your T-beam with cyanoacrylate glue.

4 Using a vise and your hobby saw, such as the one offered by X-Acto™, gently cut one 4" and one 3" piece of tubing from a 12" x ⅛" brass tube.

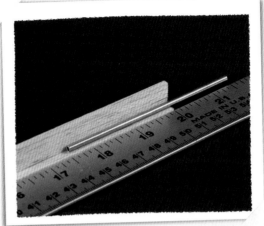

5 Measure in 2½" from the end of the T-beam. Place the end of the 4" brass tube at the mark so it extends from the T-beam; glue it along the seam. Prepare your bail by following Basic Racer I, Step 17, on page 81. Return here to Step 6 when finished.

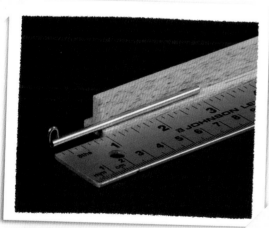

6 Using needle-nose pliers, remove the locking bar from the mousetrap. Slightly straighten the end of the bar before inserting it into the 3" piece of tube. Leaving 1" of the tube and bar assembly extending from the end of the T-beam, glue it in place.

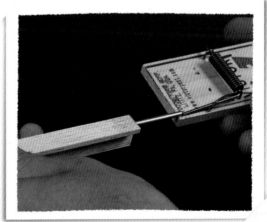

7 Insert the other end of the T-beam onto the mousetrap's cut bail, making sure the 4" tube slides under the mousetrap's spring arm at the base of the bail. Return to the Basic Racer I on page 82 and complete Steps 20 and 21. Your T-beam is complete!

The Come-Back Racer

Picture this: Your mousetrap racer begins traveling as normal, and then stops in its tracks and mysteriously travels back to you. How can you get your racer to perform this trick? The secret is that any mousetrap racer can be wound to "come back" to the racer. The trick is in the winding technique.

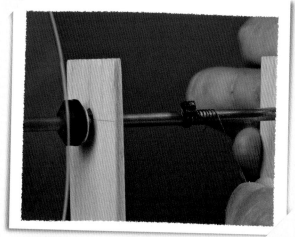

1 Begin winding the racer by turning the wheel in the same direction in which you want your racer to begin traveling—away from you.

2 When about half of the string is wound, keep the string taut, and loop it back and around the axle hook.

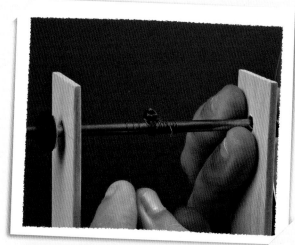

3 Begin winding the string on the other side of the hook in the opposite direction of how you want your racer to go. When the lever is released, the racer will first go forward and then reverse directions to return to the operator.

Double Trouble

Some races allow the use of two mousetraps as a power source. Just imagine how far or fast your racer could go!

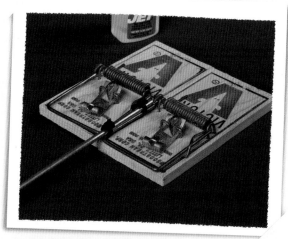

1 Remove the locking bar and accompanying staples from two Victor™-brand mousetraps. The bait plates can be removed to reduce mass, or can be left in place. Super-glue the mousetraps together side by side. Attach the 12" x ⅛" lever to the two bails with two 4" zip ties. Make sure the ties are tight and trimmed. Using a pair of needle-nose pliers, slightly straighten the non-loop end of the locking bar and then slide it all the way into one end of the brass lever arm.

2 Position the back end of the mousetraps 10¼" from the drive axle. The mousetraps should be centered between the side rails so the lever arm is positioned along the center axis of the racer. Glue the mousetraps to the deck top.

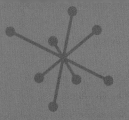

"Science may set limits to knowledge,
but should not set limits to imagination."
— Bertrand Russell

CHAPTER 5

"If the facts don't fit the theory,
change the facts."
— Albert Einstein

"Facts are meaningless. You could
use facts to prove anything that's
even remotely true!"
— Homer Simpson

Just-in-Case Techniques

Sometimes a mistake happens during construction. Or you might miss a rule for a particular contest before starting to build your racer. When problems occur, sometimes there are fixes you can use to get your mousetrap racer back on track. Many of them are detailed in this chapter.

Wire axle hooks

Should the rules for your contest require you to use a metal axle hook instead of zip tie, get a small piece of picture frame wire—approximately 3"—and follow these steps.

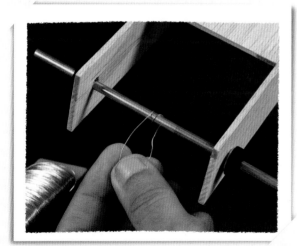

1 Loop the wire around the rear axle twice.

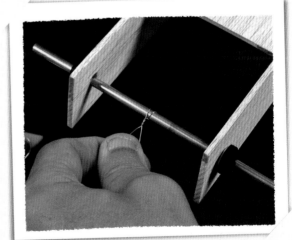

2 Twist the wire tightly.

3 Use needle-nose pliers to ensure the wire is as tight as possible.

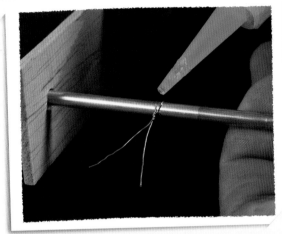

4 Glue or solder the wire in place.

5 Using wire cutters, cut the wound wire to approximately ⅛" long.

6 The completed wire axle hook.

Reversing the spring

If an error occurs and you construct your mousetrap racer with the lever on the wrong side, it may be necessary to change the direction of your mousetrap spring to avoid having to start construction from scratch.

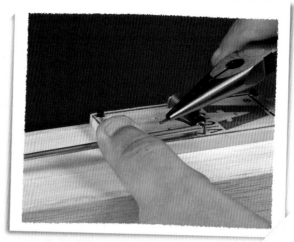

1 Using needle-nose pliers, lift the spring's arm from over the top of the brass rod.

2 Remove the brass lever arm from the cut bail arm.

3 Press down on the spring and hold it in place with your thumb. Remove the trimmed bail arm from inside the spring. Rotate the spring 180° and reassemble, holding the spring down with your thumb.

More traction

If the racing surface is too smooth, or if your racer is slipping off the starting line, it might be necessary to increase traction.

1 Cut the center section out of a balloon.

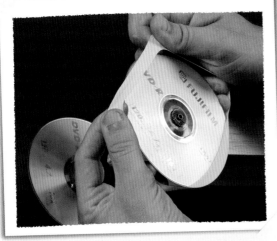

2 Stretch the cut middle section of the balloon around the diameter of the rear wheels. The balloon will overlap both sides of the CD.

3 If no balloons are available, a large rubber band can be used to help add friction to the wheel.

Attaching a lever without altering the trap

Should the rules for your contest state that the mousetrap's bail cannot be altered in any way, you still can attach a lever to it.

Once you've determined how long a lever you will be using, attach it to the mousetrap alongside the bail using two 4" zip ties. Be certain the lever rests under the spring's arm to ensure the most power possible.

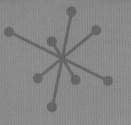

"The great tragedy of science is the slaying
of a beautiful hypothesis by an ugly fact."
— Thomas H. Huxley

CHAPTER 6

"Arithmetic is being able to count up to
twenty without taking off your shoes."
— Mickey Mouse

"Do not worry about your difficulties
in Mathematics. I can assure you
mine are still greater."
— Albert Einstein

Advanced Science Labs

For serious science students, I offer a series of labs that can help you explore in more detail many of the concepts introduced through mousetrap racers. The labs might also serve as good projects you can pursue for your school science fair. This is the first time *Lab 1: The lever's edge* has appeared in print.

Lab 1: The lever's edge

A new science fair project created by Doc Fizzix

Purpose: To understand how the length of a mousetrap racer's lever arm affects performance.

Background: Build a basic mousetrap racer and measure its average speed and travel distance through trials or experiments. Between trials, shorten the lever and reposition the mousetrap closer to the drive axle. For each shortened length of lever arm, time the racer over 5 m to determine average speed and maximum travel distance. As the lever gets shorter, the average speed over 5 m and the maximum travel distance will change.

Start with a 30-cm lever arm and shorten it by 3 cm between each trial until it is 9 cm long. Make two graphs showing the relationship between lever arm length and a mousetrap racer's motion. The first graph will show lever arm length as related to time; the second graph will show lever arm length and travel distance. The graphs will establish the relationship between the length of the lever arm and racer's performance.

Concepts and principles

Motion: Velocity and acceleration describe an object's motion. Motion involves a direction of movement through distance and time. This lab shows how the two are related.

Imagine a mousetrap racer placed at a starting line. When released, its speed increases until it reaches a maximum speed and begins decelerating until it stops. The speed changes constantly. Measuring the racer's speed at any point along the journey provides the racer's instantaneous speed. Calculating the speed over some distance gives the average speed—the distance traveled divided by the time it took to cover the distance.

Speed and velocity often are used interchangeably, but they are not the same thing. When we talk about speed, we mean how fast something is going. Velocity means how fast and in what direction. By measuring change in velocity, we get an object's acceleration.

Velocity has the following mathematical expression:

$$\text{Velocity} = \frac{\text{(distance)}}{\text{(time)}}$$

Describing force

A force is a push or pull. To change an object's state of motion, you have to apply force to it. How hard you push or pull determines how quickly you will change the state of motion. When an object changes its state of motion we say it is accelerating (or decelerating). Acceleration is proportional to the force's size. Double the force and you double acceleration.

With a mousetrap, the length of its lever arm determines the size of its pulling force. A shorter lever arm on a mousetrap racer will have more pulling force than using a longer arm. More pulling force means greater acceleration.

Force has the following mathematical expression:

Force = Mass x Acceleration

Describing torque

Torque is a force that twists or turns an object around a pivot point, changing its state of rotation. Torque depends on the size of the force and the physical point where the force acts.

Torque is applied to the mousetrap racer's wheels by pulling the wound string from the drive axle. The mousetrap's lever arm applies a force to the drive axle that causes the drive axle to pivot or rotate, causing the racer to move. By changing the drive axle's diameter or the length of the lever arm, you change the torque applied to the wheels. The torque the mousetrap spring applies to the lever is the same no matter the lever's length, but by changing the length of the lever, you change its radius and force. Shorter lever arms have more force at the tip of their levers than longer levers.

Torque has the following mathematical expression:

Torque = Force x Radius

Materials

- Basic mousetrap racer
- Stopwatch
- Meter tape or tape measure
- Long corridor or area to conduct the experiment
- Graph paper
- Masking tape (the blue painters' tape)
- Dremel tool (or hobby saw)

Hypothesis: Your hypothesis is your best educated guess as to what you think the experiment will show. Based on what you already know about mousetrap racers, write down what you think you will observe so you can compare your hypothesis to the results.

Procedure

1. Build the Basic Mousetrap-Powered Racer as shown on pages 75 through 81. Do not glue the mousetrap to the chassis. The movable mousetrap option demonstrated on page 105 is necessary for this lab.

2. Locate your starting point and place a 50-cm strip of masking tape. Carefully measure 5 m from the starting point and place another long strip of tape to mark the end of the timing distance.

3. Place the front of the mousetrap racer at the start line and have someone ready to time the racer through the 5-m distance upon its release. Release and time the racer through the 5-m distance and record the value. Allow the racer to come to rest.

4. Measure the travel distance from the start to the present location of the racer's front. Record the value.

5. Record your results for a 30-cm lever arm in Data Table 1. It is best to get an average by conducting at least three trials for each length of lever arm. Calculate the average velocity over 5 m and record below.

6. Remove the mousetrap from the chassis and the locking bar from the end of the lever arm. Use a Dremel™ tool/hobby saw to cut 3 cm off the lever. Place the locking bar into the shortened lever arm. Reposition the mousetrap on the deck-top, moving it 3 cm closer to the drive axle. Drill four new holes to attach the mousetrap at its new location.

7. Repeat Steps 4 through 6 until you have completely filled in Data Table 1 for all lever arm lengths through 9 cm.

8. Using Data Table 1, make a graph of Lever Arm Length vs. Time.

   Label your graph so Lever Arm Length is on the y-axis and Time is on the x-axis. Choose a scale so your graph will cover one whole sheet of graph paper. Plot the points for Lever Arm Length in

Data Table 1

Lever Arm Length (cm)	Time Over 5–m (s)	Average Velocity Over 5–m (m/s)	Maximum Distance (m)
30			
27			
24			
21			
18			
15			
12			
9			

centimeters and Time in seconds. Draw a best-fit line; it may not touch all points, but will show the shape of the line or curve.

9. Using Data Table 1, make a graph of Lever Arm Length vs. Maximum Distance.

Label the graph so the Lever Arm Length is on the y-axis and Maximum Distance is on the x-axis. Choose a scale so your graph will cover one whole sheet of graph paper. Plot the points for Lever Arm Length in cm and Maximum Distance in centimeters/meters. Draw a best-fit line.

Conclusion

From your graphs and data, describe the relationship between the length of the lever arm and racer performance. Compare the results to your hypothesis and discuss differences. Use the data to discuss how you would build a record-setting long-distance traveler and super-fast racer. Are there points that deviate from the norm that could show the changing relationship between the lever arm and performance? What might have happened if you continued the experiment until there was no lever arm? Explain what would happen if you made the lever arm longer.

Advanced discussion (optional): Make another graph that shows the relationship between the average velocity over 5 m and the maximum distance traveled. Is the relationship linear or exponential? Can you conclude from this graph if faster racers travel farther? Discuss your answer as it relates to your graph.

Lab 2: Chasing the mouse

Purpose: To analyze the motion of a mousetrap racer over 5 m.

Materials

- Ticker timer
- Ticker tape
- Meter stick
- Stopwatch

Ticker Tape Machine

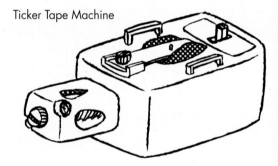

Discussion: In this lab, collect data from your mousetrap racer using a ticker timer—a device that makes marks on a ticker tape at equal intervals of time. A long piece of ticker tape will be attached to the back of your mousetrap racer. As your racer moves, the ticker timer will leave a series of marks on the tape.

Because the time between each mark is the same, a variety of variables can be measured and calculated from each mark. Analyze your racer over 5 m. After your racer has made its run, you will be measuring the distance from the first mark to each of the following marks. Velocity is the rate at which your racer is covering distance. The greater the velocity, the greater the distance covered. The average velocity is the travel distance divided by the travel time. Use Formula 1 from the list of formulas to calculate the actual velocity at each mark.

Acceleration is the rate at which your racer is changing velocity. In order to find the acceleration, you will have to first find the change in velocity between each point using Formula 2. By dividing the change in velocity for each interval, you will calculate the acceleration between each mark.

What It All Means

d = distance

v = velocity

t = time

a = acceleration

Formula # 1 :

$$\overline{v} = \frac{\Delta d}{\Delta t} \qquad \overline{v} = \frac{d_{t_r} - \iota}{\Delta_i}$$

Formula #2:

$$\overline{a} = \frac{\Delta v}{\Delta t} \qquad \overline{a} = \frac{v_{t_r} - 1}{\Delta_i}$$

Alternative approach: using a stopwatch

The stopwatch alternative

If you have a long-distance racer that travels great distances, you should not use the ticker timer. You can collect data with an alternative approach: Mark out the floor with masking tape every 1 -2 m, depending on the distance that your racer will go.

Using a stopwatch that can handle split times, walk alongside your mousetrap racer and call out the time at each mark on the floor. Have a partner record the times. Calculations are the same as with the ticker tape, but realize the distance was held constant and not the time.

The setup

1. Determine the distance over which data will be collected. Tear off enough ticker tape to cover the distance.
2. Select the frequency of the ticker timer, which determines the time between each mark. If the frequency is 10 Hz, the time between marks is $1/10$ s. If the frequency is 60 Hz, the time between marks is $1/60$ s. Record the frequency in your data table under time.
3. Label one end of the tape as the front. Thread the ticker tape through the timer and attach the front

of the tape to the rear of the racer using a small piece of tape. Position the tape so it does not tangle with the racer.

4. Place your racer at the start line. Line up the ticker timer directly behind the racer. Straighten the ticker tape behind the timer so it passes through the timer without binding. Turn the ticker timer on and then release the racer. Remove the tape from the racer after the run.

5. From the front of the ticker tape, darken each mark and label as follows: t_0, t_1, t_2, t_3, t_4, t_5, …t_n.

6. Look over Data Table 1 below and familiarize yourself with the elements you'll be measuring and calculating.

7. Measure the distance from the first mark (t_0) to the second mark (t_1) and record this as ($t_{0,1}$) distance between marks ($\Delta d_{0,1}$). Measure the distance between the second and third marks and record this as t_2 distance between marks ($\Delta d_{1,2}$). Measure the distance between each of the following marks and record as the distance

Ticker Tape Machine

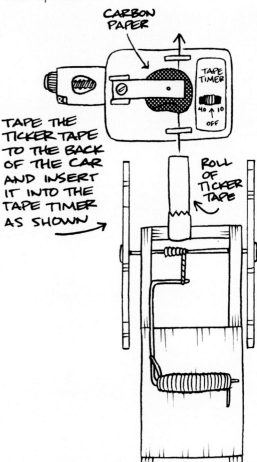

CARBON PAPER

TAPE TIMER

40 ↑ 10
OFF

TAPE THE TICKER TAPE TO THE BACK OF THE CAR AND INSERT IT INTO THE TAPE TIMER AS SHOWN →

ROLL OF TICKER TAPE

Data Table

Total Time	Change in Time	Change in Distance	Total Distance	Change in Velocity	Acceleration
$t_1 =$	$t_{0,1} =$	$\Delta d_{0,1} =$	$d_1 =$	$vf_{,1} =$	$a_{0,1} =$
$t_2 =$	$t_{1,2} =$	$\Delta d_{1,2} =$	$d_2 =$	$vf_{,2} =$	$a_{1,2} =$
$t_3 =$	$t_{2,3} =$	$\Delta d_{2,3} =$	$d_3 =$	$vf_{,3} =$	$a_{2,3} =$

between marks ($\Delta d_{2,3}$, $\Delta d_{3,4}$, $\Delta d_{4,5}$ ...Δd_n).
Note: The change in time is the difference in time between the marks, while the total time is the sum of all the time that has passed for the mark.

8. Add the change in distance between $d_{0,1}$ and record as d_1 total distance. This is the total distance from the first mark to the current mark. Add the change in distance between $d_{0,1}$ and $d_{1,2}$ record as d_2 total distance. Add the total distance between $d_{1,2}$ and $d_{2,3}$ and record as d_3 total distance. Continue until you have the total distance from each mark to the first point.

9. From equation #1 find the average change in velocity between each point or mark on your ticker tape using the following equation:

Record as change in velocity at mark $V_{0,1}$, $V_{1,2}$, $V_{2,3}$...V_n.

$$\overline{v} = \frac{\Delta d}{\Delta t}$$

$$\overline{V}_{0,1} = \frac{\Delta d_{0,1}}{\Delta t_{0,1}} \qquad \overline{V}_{1,2} = \frac{\Delta d_{1,2}}{\Delta t_{1,2}} \qquad \overline{V}_{2,3} = \frac{\Delta d_{2,3}}{\Delta t_{2,3}}$$

Record as change in velocity at mark $v_{0,1}$, $v_{1,2}$, $v_{2,3}$, ...v_n.

10: Calculate the acceleration using Formula 2 and record as follows:

$$\overline{a} = \frac{\Delta v}{\Delta t}, \qquad \overline{a}_{0,1} = \frac{\overline{V}_1 - \overline{V}_0}{\Delta t_{0,1}}$$

$$a_{1,2} = \frac{\overline{V}_2 - \overline{V}_1}{\Delta t_{1,2}}, \qquad a_{2,3} = \frac{\overline{V}_3 - \overline{V}_2}{\Delta t_{2,3}}$$

Record as acceleration between marks as $a_{0,1}$, $a_{1,2}$, $a_{2,3}$, ... a_n.

Graphing the results

In each of the following graphs, attempt to draw a best-fit line. If data is widely scattered, do not attempt to connect each dot but instead draw the best line you can that represents the shape of the dots. If you have access to a computer you can use a spreadsheet like Microsoft Excel to plot your data.

1. Graph Total Distance on the y-axis and Total Time on the x-axis.

2. Graph Velocity Final at each point on the y-axis and Total Time on the x-axis.

3. Graph Acceleration on the y-axis and Total Time on the x-axis.

Analysis

1. Identify the time intervals where your racer had the maximum positive and negative acceleration. Where did your racer have the most constant acceleration?

2. What was the racer's maximum speed over the timing distance and at what point did this occur?

3. How far was your racer pulled by its string? From the graph is it possible to determine when the string was no longer pulling the racer? Explain.

4. Compare your performance to the performance of other racers in the class and discuss how yours relates.

Lab 3: The force is against you

Purpose: To determine the amount of rolling friction acting against your mousetrap racer and the coefficient of friction.

Materials

- Ruler (a caliper works better for smaller measurements)
- Smooth ramp
- Tape measure
- Total potential energy from *Lab 7: All wound up*

Discussion

Friction acts against the motion of all moving objects. Energy is required to overcome friction and keep an object moving. Mousetrap racers start with a limited supply of energy. The energy overcomes friction and propels the racer. The less friction acting against a

moving mousetrap racer, the less energy will be lost to friction and the further the racer will travel. Air friction is a large factor with fast-moving racers, but is negligible for slow-moving distance racers. Bearing friction—two surfaces rubbing together—is the most important type of friction for slow-moving racers. The amount of friction depends on the materials doing the rubbing and the force pressing them together (Formula 3). In *Lab 3*, you will find the combined force of friction affecting your racer. The combined frictional force will be called rolling friction. The smaller the coefficient of friction, the more efficient your mousetrap racer and the greater the travel distance will be.

The setup

Finding the theoretical rolling friction requires placing your mousetrap racer on a smooth and flat board or ramp. The ramp will be elevated from one end slowly until your mousetrap racer begins to roll at constant velocity. The point or angle where that begins is where

How force works

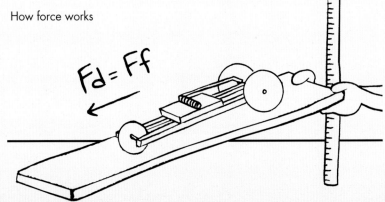

$$Fd = Ff$$

the force pulling the racer down the ramp equals the force of rolling friction acting against the racer (Formula 2). The force pulling the racer down the ramp is a combination of two forces: the force of gravity pulling straight down and the normal force of the ramp pushing back (Formula 4). As the angle of the ramp increases, the normal force decreases (Formula 5). The force of gravity remains unchanged for all angles. The difference between the two forces causes the force down the ramp to increase. The greater the angle required, the more friction there will be acting against the racer's motion. The angle is directly proportional to the force of friction or the coefficient of rolling friction (Formula 7). Lower angles are more desirable.

How Rolling Friction Works: The force pulling the racer down the ramp is equal to the force of friction acting against the racer as long as the mousetrap racer moves down the ramp at a constant velocity. In some cases, once the racer starts to move the ramp has to be lowered in order to maintain constant velocity.

Trigonometry: Trigonometry is based on simple relationships of all right triangles. Ancient mathematicians found all right triangles are proportional by ratios of their sides and angles. These ratios times the angle are known as sine, cosine, and tangent. Knowing an angle other than the right angle and any one of the sides will allow you to calculate everything else about that triangle's angles or sides.

Formula 1: $\sum F = 0$

The sum of all forces must equal zero if there is no acceleration.

Formula 2: Force Pulling = Force of Friction

Formula 3: $f_{rf} = \mu N$

Force of friction is equal to the coefficient of friction times the normal force

$$\sin\theta = \frac{h}{L}$$

Because your measurements are from a slope, you will have to use some trigonometry.

Formula 4: $f_{rf} = \sin\theta \cdot w$

The force down an angled ramp is equal to the force of friction as long as the racer rolls down the ramp with a constant velocity.

Formula 5: $N = \cos\theta \cdot w$

The normal force is the force that is perpendicular to the angled ramp.

Formula 6:

$$\mu = \frac{\sin\theta \cdot w}{\cos\theta \cdot w} = \tan\theta$$

Solving for the coefficient of friction from Formulas 3, 4 and 5.

Formula 7: $\mu = \tan\theta$

The coefficient of friction

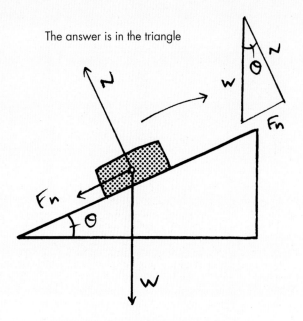

The answer is in the triangle

How it works: The angle of the ramp in this experiment forms a right triangle. The force due to gravity and the normal force of the ramp's surface cause a force directed down the ramp called Force Down. The three forces form a right triangle, which has the same angle as the base of the ramp. Knowing the angle of the base of the ramp and the weight of the racer on the ramp, we can solve for any other force including the force acting down the ramp, which is equal to the force of friction.

Let the good times roll

1. Select a long and smooth board or ramp that will not bend or flex when lifted at one end. Your racer must fit on the ramp.

2. Measure the length of the board and record this measurement as the board length (L).

3. Place your racer on the ramp and begin lifting by one end. Slowly lift until the racer begins to roll. Measure carefully and accurately the elevation of the board when the racer begins to roll and record this in the data table as the height (h). Repeat the process 5 to 10 times for more accurate results. Note: You must subtract the thickness of the board from the height. Measure both ends of the ramp to correctly calculate the height.

Data Table

Trial #	Board Length (m)	Raised Height (m)	Angle	Coefficient of Rolling Friction	Friction (N)	Starting Energy (J)	Predicted Travel Distance
1	L=	h_1=	θ_1=	μ_1=	f_1=	PE=	d_1=
2	L=	h_2=	θ_2=	μ_2=	f_2=	PE=	d_2=
3	L=	h_3=	θ_3=	μ_3=	f_3=	PE=	d_3=
4	L=	h_4=	θ_4=	μ_4=	f_4=	PE=	d_4=
Average		h=	θ=	μ=	f=		d=

4. Calculate the angle for each trial using the following equation:

$$\theta = \frac{h}{L} \sin^{-1}$$

5. From the derived formula (#7 from the list), calculate the coefficient of friction for each trial. The coefficient of friction is directly proportional to the angle of the ramp. Smaller angles translate into greater travel distance.

$$\mu = \tan\theta$$

6. If the lab is performed correctly, the force of rolling friction acting against your racer is equal to the force pulling the racer down the ramp in the elevated state. Calculate the force of friction by assuming the force down the ramp is equal to the force of friction acting against the motion of your racer. Solve for the force down the ramp using Formula 4. Be sure to use the weight of your racer in newtons. If you have the mass in kilograms, you can calculate the weight by multiplying the mass of your racer by 9.8 m/s² or find the weight by weighing your racer on a spring scale.

$$f_{rf} = \sin\theta \cdot w$$

7. Using the starting energy that you calculated in *Lab 7: All wound up*, you can calculate the predicted travel distance by using the following:

$$\text{Predicted Travel Distance} = \frac{\text{Total Potential Energy}}{\text{Rolling Friction}}$$

Lab 4: The force is against you, part II

Purpose: To determine the force of friction against your racer.

Equipment needed

- A basic mousetrap racer
- Ruler (a caliper makes smaller measurements easier)
- Stopwatch
- Meter tape
- Total potential energy from *Lab 7: All wound up*

Discussion

Mousetrap racers convert their starting energy into work. Work is done to overcome the frictional forces acting against the racer. In most cases, the largest amount of friction is the rolling friction caused by the bearings on the axles. The total work your racer will do is equal to the starting energy of your racer (calculated in *Lab 7: All wound up*.) The predicted travel distance is equal to the starting energy divided by the force of rolling friction. The less rolling friction there is, the greater the distance a racer should travel.

Calculate the friction from the actual travel distance

1. Wind up and release your racer. Measure the total travel distance. Test your result several times and calculate the average travel distance of your racer.

2. Calculate the rolling friction from the actual travel distance using the following formula:

   $$\text{Work} = \text{Force} \cdot \text{Distance}$$

   $$f_1 = \frac{PE_1}{d_1}$$

3. You are going to calculate the coefficient of friction from the following formula. Note: For mass, remove the wheels and use only the mass of the frame. It is the frame that rests on the bearings and presses the bearings' surfaces together.

   $$\mu = \frac{f}{mg}$$

Formula 8: $PE = f_{rf}d$

Work is equal to the starting energy.

Formula 9:

$$d = \frac{PE}{f_{rf}}$$

The maximum distance depends on the starting energy and the force of rolling friction.

Data Table 2

Trial #	Actual Travel Distance	Starting Energy	Friction	Coefficient of Rolling Friction
1	$d_1=$	PE=	$f_1=$	$\mu_1=$
2	$d_2=$	PE=	$f_2=$	$\mu_2=$
3	$d_3=$	PE=	$f_3=$	$\mu_3=$
4	$d_4=$	PE=	$f_4=$	$\mu_4=$
Average	$d=$		$f=$	$\mu=$

Lab 5: The spinning wheels

Purpose: To determine the amount of grip or traction your drive wheels have on the floor.

Materials

- A basic mousetrap racer
- Spring scale or force probe
- String
- Tape to lock wheels

Possible sources of more traction

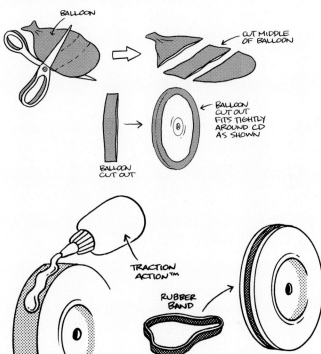

Wheel friction

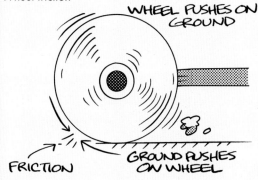

Discussion: The more grip or traction your wheels have on the floor surface, the greater the acceleration that is possible for your racer. If your racer does not have enough grip on the floor and you have too much pulling force, your wheels will spin out. If you are making a speed trap or a power pulling racer, test different materials on your wheels to make sure you have the maximum traction possible; for example, try balloons, rubber bands, different compounds, etc., on the wheels.

Once you have found the maximum traction, you can adjust the length of your mousetrap's lever arm in order to achieve the greatest possible pulling force. Shorter lever arms have greater force, resulting in more power or acceleration. Keep in mind the traction will vary from surface to surface because not all surfaces have the same grip. For example, your racer will have more grip on concrete than on ice. Because of this, you must test your racer's traction on the course you will use for your lab. In this activity, you will find the traction force and the coefficient of friction between your racer's drive wheels and the floor.

The coefficient of friction tells you how slippery two surfaces are together. The larger the coefficient of friction, the more grip or traction your racer will have with that surface.

Formulas

Formula 1: $\sum F = 0$

The sum of all forces must equal zero if there is no acceleration.

Formula 2: Force Pulling = Force of Traction

Formula 3: $f_{rf} = \mu N$

The force of traction or friction is equal to the coefficient of friction times the normal force or the force the drive wheels press on the floor.

1. With a piece of tape, lock the drive wheel(s) to prevent them from turning. The non-drive wheels should be allowed to turn freely.
2. Tie a string to the front of the racer and attach a sensitive spring scale or force probe to the string.
3. Pull the racer on the race surface at an even force and constant speed, keeping the scale or force probe parallel to the surface. Pull the racer several

times and record the readings. Calculate the average and record. The force required to drag your racer is equal to the force of traction.

4. To find the coefficient of friction between the drive wheels and the floor, you need to attach the spring scale to the drive axle and lift it directly upward until the drive wheels just lift off the table. Record this number as the force on the drive wheels. Using the formula, divide the force of traction by the force on the drive wheels.

$$\mu = \frac{f}{N}$$

Lab 6: As the wheels turn

Purpose: Find the rotational inertia of your wheels.

Materials

- A small mass (no larger than 50g; 20g recommended)
- Stopwatch
- String
- Meter stick
- Pulley setup

Discussion: Rotational inertia is the resistance of an object to efforts to change its state of rotation. The more rotational inertia a wheel has, the more torque will be required to change its state of rotation. The torque is generated from the mousetrap's lever arm. More torque means shorter lever arms, which translates into less pulling distance. With distance racers, you want the longest possible pulling distance; therefore, you want a long lever arm. In most cases, whether you are building a speed or distance racer, it is best to have wheels with as little rotational inertia as possible. The less rotational inertia a wheel has, the easier it will be to accelerate. Rotational inertia is equal to the amount of torque acting on a system divided by the angular acceleration (Formula 1). The angular acceleration is equal to the linear acceleration divided by the radius of the wheel (Formula 2). Torque equals the applied force times the radius from the point of rotation (Formula 3). Combine Formulas 1, 2, and 3 to get Formula 4.

Rotational inertia

At rest, in motion

Just as an object at rest tends to stay at rest and an object in motion tends to stay in motion, an object in a state of rotation about an axis tends to remain in that state of rotation about the same axis unless an external force or torque acts on it. Try an experiment to learn about rotational inertia: twist a barbell with the weight spaced close together and then far apart. You will definitely get a good feel for rotational inertia after this experiment.

An experiment in rotational inertia

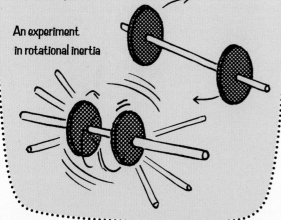

The setup

For this lab, tie a weight to a string and wrap it around the axle of each wheel. Allow the weight to fall, causing the wheel(s) to spin. Time the weight as it falls. Based on the time it takes the weight to reach the tabletop or floor, you can calculate the rotational resistance of your wheel(s). As the weight falls, gravity pulls it downward and the resistance of the wheel(s) pulls it downward. The greater the rotational resistance or inertia, the longer it will take the

131

What it all means

I = Rotational Inertia

τ = Torque

α = Angular Acceleration

a = Linear Acceleration

F = Applied Force

r = Lever Length

h = Fall Height of Mass

v_0 = Starting Falling Velocity (zero in this lab)

t = Time of Fall for Mass

a = Linear Acceleration

Formulas

Formula 1: $\tau = Fr$

Formula 2: $I = \dfrac{\tau}{\alpha}$

Formula 3: $\alpha = \dfrac{a}{r}$

Angular acceleration based on linear acceleration.

Formula 4: $I = \dfrac{Fr}{\dfrac{a}{r}}$

Formulas 1—3 combined.

Formula 5: $I = \dfrac{Fr^2}{a}$

Rotational inertia from Formula 3 based on linear acceleration.

Formula 6: $h = v_0 t + \dfrac{1}{2} at^2$

The height of fall based on an accelerating object through time.

Formula 7: $a = \dfrac{2h}{t^2}$

Solving for acceleration.

Formula 8: $I = \dfrac{Fr^2 t^2}{2h}$

Rotational inertia of a wheel based on a falling mass.

weight to fall. Formula 5 calculates the acceleration of the falling weight. Combine Formulas 4 and 5 to calculate the rotational inertia, based on the time of fall for the hanging mass. The total rotational inertia is the combination of all wheels added together.

Another way to get the job done

If your wheel(s) is (are) not glued to the axle, then you may have to design a test device to hold and measure the rotational inertia. Design a pulley apparatus that can hold each of your wheels and allows them to spin freely. The smaller the pulley or axle the string is wrapped around, the smaller the acceleration of the falling mass, which makes timing more accurate.

Another way to test

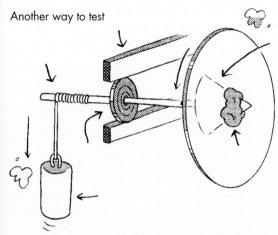

How it works: In this setup, an axle is mounted in a bearing. A clamp holds the bearing to a ring stand. A tapered cone attaches to one end of the axle. The wheel is placed onto the tapered cone and held in place with a small amount of clay. The string is wrapped around the opposite side of the axle.

Let's get spinning

Important: Steps 1–5 are only for those who test their wheels on a pulley system. If you are measuring your wheels' rotational inertia on your racer's axles, then skip to Step 6.

1. Because the pulley setup has rotational inertia of its own, you will have to calculate its rotational inertia in order to subtract it from that of your wheel.

2. Calculate the weight of your hanging mass: divide the grams by 1000 and multiply by 9.8 to determine the weight in newtons. Record in the data table. Attach the weight to the end of a string long enough to reach from the pulley to the floor or table top. Attach the other end of the string to the pulley setup and wind the string around your setup.

3. Measure the fall distance from the bottom of the hanging weight to the surface below and record this measurement as fall distance of mass (d). Measure the radius of the pulley where the string is wound and record as the pulley radius (r).

4. Allow the weight to fall while timing with a stopwatch and record the time in the data table (t). Repeat several times and record in Data Table 1. Find an average. Make sure you drop the

Data Table 1

Fall Distance of Mass	Time of Fall	Radius of Pulley	Weight of Falling Mass	Rotational Inertia of Pulley
$d_1 =$	$t_1 =$	$r_p =$	$W =$	$I_{pulley}1 =$
$d_2 =$	$t_2 =$	$r_p =$	$W =$	$I_{pulley}2 =$
$d_3 =$	$t_3 =$	$r_p =$	$W =$	$I_{pulley}3 =$
$d_4 =$	$t_4 =$	$r_p =$	$W =$	$I_{pulley}4 =$
Average	$t =$	$r_p =$	$W =$	$I_{pulley} =$

weight from the same point each time you repeat the experiment.

5. Using the following formula, calculate the rotational inertia of your pulley.

$$I = \frac{Fr^2 t^2}{2h}$$

$$I_{\text{Rotational Inertia of Wheel}} = \frac{(\text{Weight of Hanging Mass}) \cdot (\text{Radius of Pulley})^2 \cdot (\text{Time of Fall})^2}{2 \cdot (\text{Distance the mass falls})}$$

Finding the rotational inertia of your wheels

6. Depending on whether you will measure each wheel by itself or if you will measure the rotational inertia of an axle system, make a copy of Data Table 2 for each wheel or axle system for your racer. If you had to perform Steps 1–5, record the average rotational inertia from your pulley setup in Data Table 2.

7. Attach one wheel at a time to the pulley apparatus if you are measuring each wheel by itself. If you are measuring a complete axle system, then perform the following:

Attach one end of a string to the axle and the other end to a weight. The string should be long enough to reach the surface below. Calculate the weight of your hanging mass: divide the grams by 1000 and multiply by 9.8 to determine the weight in newtons. Record in Data Table 2 as W. Wind the string around the axle and measure the mass' starting position so it falls from the same height.

8. Allow the weight to fall while timing with a stopwatch and record the time (t) in Data Table 2. Repeat several times. Find an average. Make sure you drop the weight from the same point each time you repeat the experiment.

9. Using the following formula, calculate the rotational inertia of your wheel. Look carefully at the formula. It is the same as in Step 5 except this time you have to remove the rotational inertia of

Data Table 2 (front axle system or wheel 1)

Fall Distance of Mass	Time of Fall	Radius of Pulley	Weight of Falling Mass	Rotational Inertia of Pulley	Rotational Inertia of Wheel
$d_1 =$	$t_1 =$	$r_p =$	$W =$	$I_{pulley} =$	$I_{wheel}1 =$
$d_2 =$	$t_2 =$	$r_p =$	$W =$	$I_{pulley} =$	$I_{wheel}2 =$
$d_3 =$	$t_3 =$	$r_p =$	$W =$	$I_{pulley} =$	$I_{wheel}3 =$
$d_4 =$	$t_4 =$	$r_p =$	$W =$	$I_{pulley} =$	$I_{wheel}4 =$
Average	$t =$	$r_p =$	$W =$	$I_{pulley} =$	$I_{wheel} =$

Data Table 3

	Front Wheel 1 or Front Axle System	Front Wheel 2	Rear Wheel 1 or Rear Axle System	Rear Wheel 2
Rotational Inertia	$I_{f1} =$	$I_{f2} =$	$I_{f1} =$	$I_{f1} =$
Radius of Wheel	$r_{f1} =$	$r_{f2} =$	$r_{f1} =$	$r_{f1} =$

the pulley. Do not forget to subtract the resistance inertia of the pulley! If you did not use a pulley setup, plug in all variables except for the rotational inertia of the pulley.

Rotational Inertia of a Wheel or an Axle System

$$I_{\text{Rotational Inertia of Wheel}} = \frac{(\text{Weight of Hanging Mass}) \cdot (\text{Radius of Pulley})^2 \cdot (\text{Time of Fall})^2}{2 \cdot (\text{Distance the mass falls})} - I_{\text{pulley}}$$

10. Repeat for each wheel or axle system of your racer and record your results in Data Table 3.
11. Add the rotational inertia for all components.
    Total Rotational Inertia = _____ kg • m^2

Lab 7: All wound up

Purpose: Calculate the starting potential energy and find the spring coefficient.

Equipment needed

- Spring scale or a computer force probe
- Tension wheel (recommended but not needed)
- String
- Protractor
- Mousetrap
- Spring scale

Discussion: Energy has the ability to do work. A mousetrap racer's performance will depend directly on the strength of its spring. Energy stored in the wound spring is called potential energy. The amount of potential energy is the same as the work required to wind the spring. The force required to wind the spring times the distance the force was applied is equal to the work that was done on the spring (Formula 1). Because the force required to wind the spring changes and depends on how much the spring is wound, you will have to find the average force between a series of points and then calculate the work done between those marks.

The total work (or the stored potential energy) is equal to all the changes of energy between all the points added together (Formula 2). To measure the winding force, use a spring scale attached to a lever. Lift the lever and measure the force every 5 or 10 degrees. The scale must be held so the string attached to the lever is perpendicular. When the spring scale is held in different positions, it becomes inaccurate. The spring scale cannot change from the position at which it was zeroed. A tension wheel allows the spring scale to remain in one position, producing more accurate results.

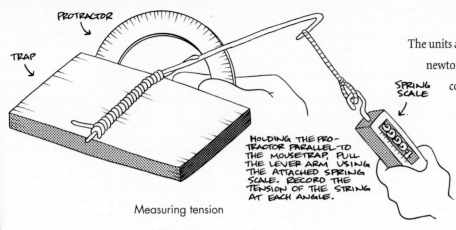

PROTRACTOR

TRAP

SPRING SCALE

HOLDING THE PRO-
TRACTOR PARALLEL TO
THE MOUSETRAP, PULL
THE LEVER ARM USING
THE ATTACHED SPRING
SCALE. RECORD THE
TENSION OF THE STRING
AT EACH ANGLE.

Measuring tension

The setup

Holding the protractor parallel to the mousetrap, pull the lever arm using the attached spring scale. Record string tension at each angle.

The distance the average force was applied is equal to the angle of the measurement in radians times the length of the measuring lever arm. If you are using a tension wheel, then the radius of the wheel is the measuring lever arm (Formula 3). Formula 4 allows you to convert from degrees to radians.

For a spring stretched or compressed longitudinally, Hooke's Law says the force is equal to the spring constant times the stretching or compressing displacement. However, a mousetrap spring does not stretch longitudinally; it is a torsion spring and winds up. A torsion spring needs a different formula (Formula 5). Torque must be applied to the spring to wind it and the displacement is measured in radians (Formula 6).

The units associated with the spring constant become newtons • meters/radians. For a spring that compresses or stretches in a linear direction, the total potential energy is half the spring constant times the displacement squared (Formula 7). For a torsion spring, the angle in radians substitutes for displacement (Formula 8).

Tools of the trade: tension wheel

A tension wheel directs the pulling force in the same direction as the spring is wound, which prevents the scale from having to be rezeroed as its direction of pull changes. Degree markings make it easy to measure force and angle.

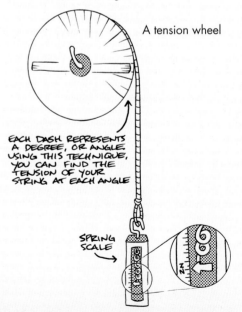

A tension wheel

EACH DASH REPRESENTS
A DEGREE, OR ANGLE.
USING THIS TECHNIQUE,
YOU CAN FIND THE
TENSION OF YOUR
STRING AT EACH ANGLE

SPRING SCALE

Spring scale

How it works: As the wheel is turned clockwise, the spring on the mousetrap is compressed. The value of the spring constant depends on the material from which the spring is made, the diameter of the wire, the diameter of the coil, and the number of coils.

A spring scale

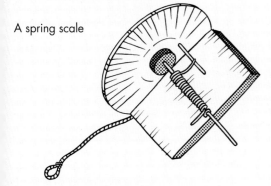

Pulling your weight

1. Use either a spring scale or a force probe to measure the spring's tension at different points during its travel. Start by attaching a string—about 20 cm long—to the end of the mousetrap's extended lever arm. The point where the string is attached must extend past the edge of the mousetrap's base so measurements can be taken from 0 to 180 degrees without interference. Attach the spring scale to the other end of the string. Hold or attach a protractor to the mousetrap so that the center point of the protractor is in the middle of the spring and the zero degree point is lined up with the starting point of the relaxed lever arm.

Formulas

What it all means

W = Work

F = Force

d = Displacement

k = Linear Spring Constant

$\varkappa$ = Torsion Spring Constant

x = Spring Displacement

τ = Torque

θ = Angle

PE = Potential Energy

Formula 1: $W = F \cdot d$
Work formula used with a constant (non-changing) force.

Formula 2: $W = \int_0^\pi F(x)\, d(x)$
Work formula used with a changing force like a mousetrap spring.

Formula 3: $d = \theta r$
A formula to calculate the linear distance of travel for a wheel.

Formula 4: $\text{degrees} \times \dfrac{\pi}{180°} = \theta$
A formula used to change degrees into radians.

Formula 5: $F = -kx$
Hooke's Law. Force of a stretched or compressed spring.

Formula 6: $\tau = k\theta$
From Hooke's Law. Used to calculate the torque from a torsional spring.

Formula 7: $PE = \dfrac{1}{2} kx^2$
Potential energy of a stretched or compressed spring.

Formula 8: $PE = \dfrac{1}{2} \kappa\theta^2$
Potential energy of a stretched or compressed torsion spring.

2. Start at 0° and pull up on the lever arm with the spring scale until the lever arm just lifts up from the base of the mousetrap. Record this measurement as the starting force. Continue to pull up on the spring scale, stopping at every 5° or 10°. Record the tension at each point in the data table. You must keep the scale perpendicular to the lever arm at each point you measure.

3. Calculate the change in radians for each angle and record them in the data table. If each measurement was made at the same increment (e.g. every 5°) you can use the same change in radians for all angles. Use the following method to calculate the change in radians:

$$\Delta\theta_1 = (\text{degrees}_1 - \text{degrees}_0) \times \frac{\pi}{180°}$$

$$\Delta\theta_2 = (\text{degrees}_2 - \text{degrees}_1) \times \frac{\pi}{180°}$$

Data Table 1

Angle	Tension	Change in Radians	Total Radians	Change in Displacement	Total Displacement
5	$F_0=$	$\Delta\theta_0=0$	$\theta_0=0$	$\Delta d_0=0$	$d_0=0$
10	$F_1=$	$\Delta\theta_1=$	$\theta_1=$	$\Delta d_1=$	$d_1=$
15	$F_2=$	$\Delta\theta_2=$	$\theta_2=$	$\Delta d_2=$	$d_2=$
20	$F_3=$	$\Delta\theta_3=$	$\theta_3=$	$\Delta d_3=$	$d_3=$
25	$F_4=$	$\Delta\theta_4=$	$\theta_4=$	$\Delta d_4=$	$d_4=$
180	$F_{36}=$	$\Delta\theta_{36}=$	$\theta_{36}=$	$\Delta d_{36}=$	$d_{36}=$

Data Table 2

Spring Constant	Torque	Change in Energy Potential	Total Potential Energy
$k_0=0$	$\tau_0=$	$\Delta PE_0=0$	$PE_0=0$
$k_1=$	$\tau_1=$	$\Delta PE_1=$	$PE_{0-1}=$
$k_2=$	$\tau_2=$	$\Delta PE_2=$	$PE_{0-2}=$
$k_3=$	$\tau_3=$	$\Delta PE_3=$	$PE_{0-3}=$
$k_4=$	$\tau_4=$	$\Delta PE_4=$	$PE_{0-4}=$
$k_{36}=$	$\tau_{36}=$	$\Delta PE_{36}=$	$PE_{0-36}=$
Average Spring Constant			Total PE_{0-36}

4. Measure the length of the lever arm from the spring to the point where the scale was attached. Record this as the radius. Calculate the change in displacement, also known as the arc length, for each angle using the following formula. If each measurement was made at the same increment, you can use the same arc length (displacement) for all angles.

$$\Delta d_1 = \Delta\theta_1 r \quad \Delta d_2 = \Delta\theta_2 r \quad \Delta d_3 = \Delta\theta_3 r$$

5. Calculate the total displacement for each angle by adding each of the previous changes in displacement to the next.

6. Calculate the change in potential energy for each point using the following method: Multiply the average force between the starting and ending points with the change in distance. Add each change in PE values together in order to find the total potential energy from the column. This added value should be the energy your vehicle starts with before it is released.

$$\Delta PE_{0,1} = \frac{F_0 + F_1}{2} \cdot \Delta d_1$$

$$\Delta PE_{1,2} = \frac{F_1 + F_2}{2} \cdot \Delta d_2$$

$$\Delta PE_{2,3} = \frac{F_2 + F_3}{2} \cdot \Delta d_3$$

7. Calculate the spring constant for each change in angle. The spring on a mousetrap is a torsion spring—it coils instead of stretching. Use the following equation to calculate the spring constant: $\tau = \kappa\theta$. Torque is equal to the spring constant times the angle in radians. Torque is calculated from the force applied to a lever arm times the length of the lever arm. $\tau = Fr_{\text{lever arm}}$. Subtract the starting torque in order to find the actual change in torque for each change in angle. Total each spring constant and find an average.

$$\kappa = \frac{\tau}{\theta}$$

$$\kappa_1 = \frac{(F_1 - F_0)r_{\text{arm length}}}{\theta_{0,1}}$$

$$\kappa_2 = \frac{(F_2 - F_1)r_{\text{arm length}}}{\theta_{1,2}}$$

$$\kappa_3 = \frac{(F_3 - F_2)r_{\text{arm length}}}{\theta_{2,3}}$$

Graphing the results

In each of the following graphs, attempt to draw best-fit lines. If data is widely scattered, do not attempt to connect each dot but instead draw the best shape of the dots. If you have access to a computer, you can use a spreadsheet program like Microsoft Excel to plot your data.

1. Graph Pulling Force on the y-axis and the Displacement on the x-axis.
2. Graph Torque on the y-axis and Angle in Radians on the x-axis.

Analysis

1. The slope from your graph of Torque vs. Angle represents the spring constant. Does the slope change or remain constant? Do you have an ideal spring that follows Hooke's Law?
2. What does the slope of the line from each of your graphs tell you about the strength of your spring as compared to other students' springs?
3. Calculate the area under all parts of the best-fit line using the Torque vs. Angle graph. This number represents the potential energy you are starting with. The larger the number, the more energy available to do work. This number should be close to the total potential energy calculated from Data Table 2. How does the slope compare to the number in the data table?
4. How do your potential energy results compare to other results from your class? Discuss.

Lab 8: How far can I go?

Purpose: To determine pulling distance, power output, and mechanical advantage.

Materials

- Ruler (a caliper or micrometer makes smaller measurements easier)
- Stopwatch
- Meter Tape
- Total Potential Energy from *Lab 7: All wound up*

Discussion: The pulling distance is the measurement from where the vehicle starts to where the pulling force on the drive axle ends. In this lab, you will calculate how far the lever arm will pull your racer. Once you have predicted the pulling distance, you will then measure and time the actual pulling distance in order to find the power rating. The pulling distance does not tell you how far your racer will travel, only how far it will be pulled by the lever arm. The distance your racer is pulled is directly proportional to the size of the drive wheels and the length of string wrapped around the drive axle. The travel distance is inversely proportional to the size of the drive axle. The larger the drive wheel(s), the greater the pulling distance. The more string that can be pulled off the drive axle, the greater the pulling distance. The larger the drive axle, the shorter the pulling distance. To get more string wound around the drive axle, you can do one of the following: use a smaller diameter drive axle or extend the length

Formulas

Pulling Distance = Number of Turns · $2\pi r_{wheel}$

Number of Turns = $\dfrac{\text{Length of String}}{2\pi r_{axle}}$

Pulling Distance = $\dfrac{\text{Length of String} \cdot r_{wheel}}{r_{axle}}$

$P_I = \dfrac{PE_{total}}{\Delta T_I}$

Power is the rate at which energy is being used.

of the mousetrap's lever arm and then place the trap further from the drive axle.

Calculate pulling distance from the number of turns your wheel makes times the circumference of your wheel. The number of turns that your wheel will make depends on the length of string wound around the pulling axle divided by the circumference of the drive axle. By putting the first two formulas together, you can predict the pulling distance.

Power output: Power is the rate of work. Your racer will convert stored potential energy from the wound spring into work to overcome friction. The rate at which your mousetrap car converts this stored energy into work is your racer's power rating. You will calculate the power rating by dividing the starting energy by the time

through the pulling distance (Formula 4). As a general rule of thumb, higher power ratings mean less efficiency and less overall travel distance. A good mousetrap car designed for distance should have a low power rating.

Getting the measurements

1. Use a caliper or micrometer to measure and calculate the average diameter of the drive axle. Measure the drive axle without string on it and then with wound-up string, as it would be before a race. It is important the string be wound evenly. Add the two measurements together and divide by 2 to get an average diameter. Calculate the average radius from the average diameter.

   Average Drive Axle Diameter = _____ m

   Average Drive Axle Radius = _____ m

2. Use a caliper or a ruler to measure the diameter of the drive wheel(s) and record the diameters as well as the radii.

   Drive Wheel(s) Diameter = _____ m

   Drive Wheel(s) Radius = _____ m

How It Works:

A caliper is used to measure the thickness of the drive axle in order to calculate the diameter. For a more accurate calculation of the diameter of the drive axle, two measurements will be taken: with and without string.

3. Measure only the length of string normally pulled from the drive axle. Important: If there is more string attached to the lever arm than is needed, you may have to wind the string around the drive axle and then mark the string where it starts and ends with respect to the lever arm's travel range.

   String Length = _____ m

4. Calculate the pulling distance using the following formula:

$$\text{Pulling Distance} = \frac{\text{Length of String } \times r_{wheel}}{r_{axle}}$$

5. Calculate the mechanical advantage from the following formula:

$$\frac{F_{\text{Force string applies to drive axle}}}{F_{\text{Force of wheel to road}}} = \frac{r_{\text{radius of wheel}}}{r_{\text{radius of drive axle}}} = \frac{d_{\text{Distance vehicle is pulled by lever arm}}}{d_{\text{String on axle}}} = IMA$$

Part II: Determine power output

6. Time your vehicle over the pulling distance. Perform 3 to 5 trials. Record your data.

7. Calculate the power by dividing the total starting energy from *Lab 2: Chasing the mouse* by the time over the pulling distance. Compare your value to other vehicles' power.

$$P_1 = \frac{PE_{total}}{\Delta t_1} \qquad P_2 = \frac{PE_{total}}{\Delta t_2}$$

Graphing the results

Make a graph of the Power Rating vs. Total Travel Distance. Put Power Rating on the x-axis and Total Travel Distance on the y-axis.

Make a graph of Pulling Distance vs. Mechanical Advantage. Put Mechanical Advantage on the x-axis and Pulling Distance on the y-axis.

Analysis

Describe any relationship that might exist between power rating and travel distance.

Describe any relationship that might exist between wheel-to-axle ratio and pulling distance.

Data Table 1

Pulling Distance	Total Travel Distance	Time Over Pulling Distance	Starting Energy from Lab 2	Power Output
$d_1 =$	Total d_1	t_1	PE =	$P_1 =$
$d_2 =$	Total d_2	t_2	PE =	$P_2 =$
$d_3 =$	Total d_3	t_3	PE =	$P_3 =$